# FOUL DEEDS & SUSPICIOUS DEATHS
# AROUND ROCHDALE

Foul Deeds and Suspicious Deaths Around

# ROCHDALE

John Cole

**Wharncliffe Books**

# For Sue

First published in Great Britain in 2007 by
Wharncliffe Books
*an imprint of*
Pen & Sword Books Ltd
47 Church Street
Barnsley
South Yorkshire
S70 2AS

© John Cole 2007

ISBN: 978 184560 10 2

A CIP catalogue record for this book is available from
the British Library

Typeset in Plantin and ITC Benguiat by
Mousemat Design Limited

Printed and bound in Great Britain by CPI UK

Pen & Sword Books Ltd incorporates the imprints of
Pen & Sword Aviation, Pen & Sword Maritime,
Pen & Sword Military, Wharncliffe Local History,
Pen and Sword Select, Pen and Sword Military Classics
and Leo Cooper.

For a complete list of Pen & Sword titles please contact
PEN & SWORD BOOKS LIMITED
47 Church Street, Barnsley, South Yorkshire,
S70 2AS, England
E-mail: enquiries@pen-and-sword.co.uk
Website: www.pen-and-sword.co.uk

# Contents

# Acknowledgements

Many thanks to all those who helped put this book together:

Robert Harding and Christopher Summerville for their editorial suport, Duncan Broady at the Greater Manchester Police Museum for access to the collection and permission to reproduce the 'police' photos in Chapters 10 and 15.

Richard Catlow, Claire Mooney and Chris Lloyd at the *Rochdale Observer* for access to their files.

Staff at the Lancashire Record Office, Preston.

Peggy Seeger for permission to produce the lyrics reproduced in Chapter 7 from Ewan MacColl's *Dirty Old Town* (words, music Ewan MacColl, © EMI). Full lyrics can be found in the *Essential Ewan MacColl Songbook* (Music Sales, USA) and information on Ewan can be found on the website, www.pegseeger.com.

Special thanks to:

Peggy Seeger for her kind words.

Staff at the amazing Rochdale Local Studies Library, for access to the collections, for support and advice; to Shirley Warburton for finding the Dirty Old Town story, to Pam Godman for the scans and to Joy Hopwood for the work on 'The Adventure of the Steel Corset'.

Julian Jefferson on behalf of Touchstones and Link4Life for permission to use all the wonderful illustrations from the Local Studies collection (which is every picture bar the police photos credited to the Greater Manchester Police Museum).

Rochdale Local Studies library can be accessed on-line at: www.Link4Life.org and click on Arts and Heritage.

Finally, readers should note that all images used in this book were provided by the Rochdale Local Studies Library collection, except for Chapter 15, 1 and Chapter 15, 3, which were provided by the Greater Manchester Police Museum.

# Introduction

## Rochdale: A Town and its People

Rochdale is an old town, surrounded by brooding Pennine hills
and wild open moorland, the historic centre of a vast parish and
manor. Stone Age and Bronze Age finds are common in the area;
the Romans and Saxons were here and the town was already old
when, in 1251, a market was established by Royal Charter. A
year later, 'Henry III granted the Knights of St John of Jerusalem
the right to try thieves and erect a gallows at Butterworth in the
parish of Rochdale.'

It was by the ancient name of *Rechedham* that Rochdale was
referred to in the *Domesday Book*, implying a connection with
the sub-Roman administrative area of Rheged and its northern
capital near modern Carlisle.

In the uplands around Rochdale are a maze of tracks and
paths created as merchants travelled north and east taking to the
high ground, skirting marshes and meres, and forging routes
between Lancashire and Yorkshire through some of the most
inhospitable land in England. Their packhorses laden with
coarse woollen cloth produced by local farmer-weavers, these
merchants established trading links throughout Britain and then
to France, Germany, Holland and Portugal.

Cloth-makers laboured in tiny smallholdings scattered over
11 square miles of bleak moorland. For them life was hard. One
visitor to the area referred to the farmer-weavers as, 'a sturdy
mountain breed' but few travellers lingered here for long.

Such spiritual life as existed revolved around the parish church
of St Chad, high on a hill overlooking the centre of Rochdale. The
church first appears in written records in 1194 but its Saxon wall
speaks of a far earlier origin. Few vicars of Rochdale Parish lived
in the area, preferring the more refined attractions of London and
the South and leaving any actual ministering to a succession of
poorly paid curates. As a result, local people were as likely to
believe in witches and ghosts as the Holy Spirit.

*St Chad's Parish Church: the spiritual centre of the parish.*
Rochdale Local Studies Library collection

The parish and manor of Rochdale shared powers of local taxation and justice between them. It was therefore by no accident that the stocks were strategically placed outside the doors of St Chad's church. According to one vicar the stocks were, 'exceedingly well and regularly used' . . . as indeed were the gallows operated by the Knights Templar at Butterworth.

*The stocks outside St Chad's Church.* Rochdale Local Studies Library collection

Women were deemed to be, 'exempt from the stocks by virtue of their gender' and so a ducking-stool was provided, 'for their special benefit' to plunge them into the icy waters of the River Roch. According to local legend, the most frequent victim of the ducking-stool was Betty Brindle who, in the early eighteenth century, asserted, 'in front of a lively female audience in the *Roebuck Hotel* that women should by natural right sit as Judges and MPs'. This proved too radical a concept for the male leaders of Church and State, who punished her accordingly.

Applying the letter of these harsh laws was the Lord of the Manor and a dozen or so members of the local gentry. This select group belonged to merchant families who, having made a fortune in wool trading, built imposing wooden halls in and around the town.

The local way of life remained unaltered for centuries, the economy still based around agriculture and small-scale domestic spinning and weaving. However, by 1600 the wooden halls of the merchants and traders were being replaced by stone structures as grey and solid as the Pennine hills. Then, in and around the Pennines, began the most cataclysmic period of change that Britain has ever undergone. It is no exaggeration to say that the way that the world is now is due to events that happened within a 10-mile radius of Rochdale.

Water-powered corn mills on the fast-flowing Pennine streams were converted to woollen spinning; then as steam power took over in the late seventeenth century, factories were relocated from the countryside to the centres of population, the market towns and villages. The Industrial Revolution had begun.

Rochdale's growth was staggering. From a population of 10,000 in 1801, the town had 17,000 inhabitants by 1821, 24,000 in 1841, rising to 70,000 by 1881.

With this increase in population came huge social problems. Speculative builders threw up hovels on any available piece of land, creating instant slums. There was no sanitation. Disease was rife; the average life expectancy plunged to 21; hunger and unemployment haunted all but the wealthiest. Food riots became commonplace and troops were regularly brought in to quell the unrest.

On the positive side, local people pioneered nationwide advances in fields as diverse as public health, education and trades-unionism. And of course it was here in 1844 that a group of social and political activists devised the principles that even now govern the Co-operative movement and its 700 million members worldwide.

Less positively, crime spiralled way beyond the control of the Manor Court and its handful of decrepit nightwatchmen, and

the authorities lost control of the town. The establishment of a
Police Commission in 1825 did not significantly improve public
safety. The poorly paid watchmen (or beadles) appointed under
the Rochdale Police Act were as likely to be involved in the
committing of petty crime as the detection of it.

Rochdale was to remain a hotbed of political activity for
many years, but for every expression of public discontent in the
area there was an individual crime of passion, a fatal drunken
brawl, a garrotting, a bloody robbery and a terrible murder.

The *Foul Deeds* described here owe much to the geography
and social development of the area. This is not to excuse those
who perpetrated these shocking crimes, but it does provide a
fascinating context.

In the nineteenth century much of the crime was committed
by people crammed together cheek-by-jowl in towns and cities
but even the rural deeds of murder, forgery, highway robbery
and suicide related here have a gritty northern feel to them.

And as we encounter more recent crimes, there is still a
strong evocation of place, making all the tales told here very
specifically *Rochdale Foul Deeds and Suspicious Deaths*.

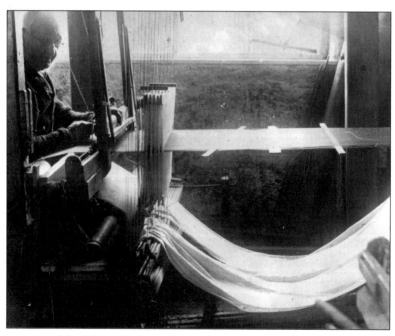

*A local handloom weaver.* Rochdale Local Studies Library collection

# CHAPTER 1

# Tales of the Supernatural

Memories of murders and other foul deeds were often handed down through the generations as folk tales and ghost stories. Legends passed on by people who believed in witches, spirits, sprites and goblins became so interwoven that it is often impossible to pinpoint their origins. Some cautionary tales acted as warnings to the young, others were invented to deter investigation into criminal activities, yet others were simply products of superstition or beliefs.

Unsurprisingly for a town with such a long continuous history, Rochdale is rich in accounts of ancient murders, Satanism, witchcraft and ghostly apparitions. The most famous of these stories – the legend of Clegg Hall and its Boggart – follows, after a brief look at some more bizarre tales of the supernatural. This tour of the distant past will provide a gentle introduction to the mayhem to come in later chapters.

At first acquaintance, the earliest surviving local legend – that of The Goblin Builders – seems pointless: a myth without moral or purpose. One genuine historical figure features in the story. He was Gamel, a Saxon Thane, a comparatively unimportant nobleman who was fortunate enough to hold land in the area under King Edward the Confessor, 'with no taxes or customs due'. This allowed him a free hand in building a castle, a church or a fortified manor house. There is not a shred of evidence to indicate that he did any of those things, although the local names Castleton and Castlemere suggest that somebody at some time built a fortification in the area.

However, the legendary Gamel, as opposed to the real one, set about erecting a mythical church in or around 1086, 400 years after the probable foundation of the genuine article.

This task proved unexpectedly difficult. Piles of timber and huge stones were gathered for the foundations and stakes were driven into the soft earth on the low-lying area around the present Town Hall. And yet, in a single night, everything, timbers, staves and rocks, was miraculously transported up the hill to the site of the present parish church.

A furious Gamel summoned the local gentry and it was decided that a priest should bless the original site. Following the blessing, the building materials were laboriously carried back downhill; night fell, a new day dawned and . . .

Anyway, to cut a long shaggy-dog story short, the culprits were eventually identified as, yes, goblins who intervened again and again until a weary Gamel finally gave up and built his church, with the help of the goblins, high on the hill where it stands today, 122 steps above the town centre.

It may seem pointless but in fact the legend of the Goblin Builders can tell us a lot about old Rochdale. The terrain adjacent to the River Roch was marshy, hence the name Castlemere. The meres may have dried out in summer, but the land certainly would not have supported a major structure like a church. Perhaps the legend recalls an unsuccessful attempt at building there; but whether deterred by goblins or drainage, no major construction took place on the site for centuries after Gamel had his brush with the supernatural.

As well as goblins that built churches, Rochdale also possessed a ghostly rabbit, which hopped around the area known as the Baum, near St Mary's Church on Toad Lane. However, as this 'Baum Rabbit' is neither evil nor blood-curdling, it probably doesn't belong in a book of *Foul Deeds*.

Far more sinister was the widespread practise of, or at least belief in, witchcraft. The earliest recorded local example of 'witch haunting' dates from 1597 when Alice Brerely of Castleton was granted a pardon, after being sentenced to death for killing James Kershaw and Robert Scholefield, 'by witchery'.

Again in Castleton, in October 1641, an Alice Schofield was bound over to appear at Manchester Quarter Sessions accused of:

*Devilish Practises with a sieve and a pair of sheers for the purpose of discovering who had stoulen a certain sheepe of the goods and chattel of John Newbold and a hen from John Feilden of Belfield and also to ascertain whether Jane Brearley of Ogden were with child and Mary the daughter of the aforesaid John Feilden were with child.*

Amazing what you can do with a sieve and a pair of sheers.

It was not just the poor and superstitious who believed in the Devil and all his works. In 1696 Rochdale born and educated

Zachary Taylor published his *The Devil Turned Causist*, in which he claimed that Catholic priests, 'finding that members of their congregation were turning to Protestantism, were creating myths of possession by evil spirits in order to persuade the gullible to return to the fold'.

Taylor described in minute detail an exorcism performed on Thomas Ashton, a weaver said to be possessed, during which the priest, 'brought forth a devil called Loll'. As part of the exorcism the priest, for some reason known only to himself, felt it would be useful to 'call the devil by name of a cursed toad' but unfortunately was unable complete the spell as 'he could not for the life of him remember the Latin word for toad'.

This was sufficient provocation for a baffled Zachary Taylor to apply for a warrant for the priest's arrest and the surreal episode ends with the priest hightailing it out of Lancashire with

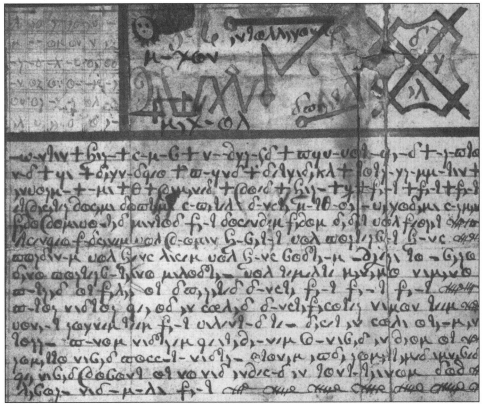

*The witch charm containing the 'Number of the Beast, 666' found at Healey.*
Rochdale Local Studies Library collection

the army in pursuit.

Many local people devised their own defences against witches and evil spirits. In 1876 workmen demolishing a barn in Healey found in the roof timbers an old wooden box containing a coded witch charm. In the top right-hand corner was a magic square dedicated to the sun, on which numbers were represented by letters from the Greek alphabet. Any six combinations in the square, if read in a straight line and added together, made 666 – 'the number of the beast'.

The word *Tetragrammaton* (the Hebrew name for God that is too holy to be spoken aloud) was followed in the text by the imprecation: 'If there be a bewitcher or a demon dwelling in or inhabiting this person, this place or this thing, I exorcise it to depart without any disturbance, trouble or the least tumult, in the name of the Father, the Son and the Holy Ghost.'

Such charms were not uncommon and were often targeted at specific individuals, although there was a world of difference between the concept of demonic possession and the activities of local 'wise women' even if the women themselves were often branded as witches. Over the centuries, thousands of women produced herbal potions and remedies for all ailments and conditions. They dispensed their wisdom as readily as their medicines and were regarded with awe; treated with deference by some and suspicion and jealousy by others. Consequently no small number of wise women added a curse or two to their repertoire.

One such character was Jane Wenham, one of the last and certainly one of the most famous women to be tried for witchcraft in England. Jane lived much of her life in Walkern, Hertfordshire and was put on trial for curing a sixteen-year-old girl's injured knee. During the hearing, Jane failed to say the Lord's Prayer without hesitation, repetition, or deviation and was deemed to possess more cats than was appropriate for a God-fearing woman. Clearly she was a witch.

The jury sentenced her to death but she was pardoned by the judge and allowed to live out her life on a nearby estate. The story is well known. However, there is a persistent local legend that links Jane Wenham to Rochdale. Eighteenth century historian William Robertson in his *History of Rochdale Past and Present* dedicated forty pages to Jane's upbringing. He described her early life in Rochdale, her close contacts with the vicar, Henry Pigot, her elopement and marriage and her eventual relocation to Walkern.

The legacy of women like Jane Wenham was passed down through the generations. Only 100 years or so ago, Rochdale wise woman, Nell Racker, gained a formidable reputation. Ellen Isherwood was born at Pigslee, near Walmersley, Bury, on 12 October, 1846. The family moved to Milnrow in 1847 or 1848. Sometime in the 1890s Ellen married her second husband, John

*Nell Racker; the twentieth-century Rochdale 'Wise Woman'.*

Rochdale Local Studies Library collection

Wallace and the couple moved to a small cottage in the Belfield area of Rochdale.

There, Ellen Wallace became commonly known as Nell Racker, a name she loathed. People who visited her for treatment or consultations crept through the tangled garden, glancing nervously at the assortment of kettles, pans and teapots, which were strung amongst the tree branches. After tapping at the door they would enter the house, noting the unfamiliar odours and bunches of herbs hung from a cluster of racks on the ceiling. It was these racks that bequeathed Ellen the nickname she despised.

Nell Racker would, for a fee, dispense arcane knowledge and potions, set a broken arm, or arrange to attend a birth. She was a registered midwife.

Like many a wise woman before her, Ellen Wallace discretely offered 'extra' services. Abortions were not legally available at the time and in 1917, following a charge of 'negligence' she was struck off the Midwives' Register. She was, however, still visited regularly by locals wanting their fortunes told or by friends who came to listen to her tales of ghosts and witches.

There was a large audience for such stories. As the *Rochdale Times* noted in 1889, belief in the supernatural was widespread: 'Many superstitions are still prevalent amongst large numbers of people in the town and parish. Whole areas are deemed to be haunted.' Healey Dell had its own 'Fairies' Chapel' and the area gloomily called 'The Doldrums' above Milnrow was haunted by a witch's familiar, a black cat. At the end of the nineteenth century the whole of Dawson Square off Rope Street was abandoned because residents reported seeing the ghost of murder victim Annie McKenna gliding through the walls. (See Chapter 10)

It is a historical fact that during the English Civil War a company of Roundheads led by Colonel Roseworm were camped high on Blackstone Edge. Even in summer this can be a forbidding place. Traveller and writer Daniel Defoe was beaten back by a blizzard as he attempted to cross over into Yorkshire . . . in July!

So life was no bed of roses for the Roundheads, especially as one of their tasks was to upgrade a stone causeway making it fit to haul munitions up the steep gradient. Possibly this explains the temperament of a ghost that haunted the nearby Rake Inn, a handsome cavalier who wandered around the corridors laughing uproariously.

The Rake Inn, *Littleborough; haunted by the ghost of the 'Laughing Cavalier'.*
Rochdale Local Studies Library collection

Such tales persist to the present day. The area that witnessed the activities of the ghostly rabbit is still known as the Baum, derived from the word balm, a healing herb. The old church of St Mary stood there until 1909 when it was replaced by the current building.

During the reconstruction there was some encroachment on the graveyard and scores of coffins were relocated into three deep trenches. Since the new market opened in 1975 there have been numerous sightings of a male apparition drifting across the Baum, through the walls of the market into the fish section and the canteen before disappearing in the far corner of the building.

Most tales of haunting in the area, however, relate to the activities of boggarts. These were mischievous spirits whose behaviour resembled poltergeist. Boggarts would 'rearrange furniture, break crockery, scare the children and emit strange noises'. If not treated with due respect they could turn nasty; changing shape and wreaking havoc, transformed into animals or fabulous beasts.

Ghosts of people were also called boggarts, and the word became applied locally to almost any ghostly presence or super-natural phenomenon.

Amongst the most disruptive of these unruly spirits was the Gristlehurst Boggart.

So rowdy was this unwanted visitor that a suitable sacrifice had to be made to appease and finally exorcise it. Accordingly, a cock was buried with a stake thrust through it. Exit boggart . . . but a fowl deed nevertheless.

Undoubtedly the most famous boggart, regionally as well as locally, belonged to Clegg Hall. Many swear to having experienced psychic phenomena in the vicinity. Scores claim to have seen the ghost. Some sightings even made the local press. The *Rochdale Times* of 12 April 1890 described how a local man walking the canal towpath from Hollingworth Lake late at night, 'was startled by a strange apparition. It was a great shadowy form, apparently intangible, which to his horror began to chase him along the bank and over the canal bridge until he eventually reached safety.'

Clegg Hall is that sort of building, the perfect setting for a tale of murder and haunting. The historical facts relating to the building are these: early deeds reveal that in the reign of King Stephen (reigned 1135–54) Bernulf de Clegg and his wife Quinelda built a house on the site of the present hall. By the thirteenth century the land in the area was passed from the De Cleggs to the Belfields, but it was Theophilus Assheton who had the current stone hall built in around 1610.

A survey of the Manor of Rochdale completed in 1626 described Clegg Hall as 'a faire capital messuage built with free stone with gardens, stables, courts, orchards, gardens, foulds, fish ponds and pigeon houses'.

All of which sounds idyllic, but even then Clegg Hall must have looked austere and forbidding. Its external details were architecturally advanced for the Rochdale area, but its heavy 'double pile' construction and its isolated situation lent it a sinister aspect.

In 1801 the Rochdale Canal was cut immediately in front of the hall, and in 1810 Joseph Fenton of Crimble Hall built a flannel mill on an adjacent parcel of land. Weavers' cottages were added in 1817 and in order to serve this increased population, part of Clegg Hall was converted into a pub. Originally called the *Black Sloven* after the landlord's favourite racehorse, pub and hall deteriorated until, in 1869, by then known as the *Hare and Hounds*, the inn had its license revoked.

As the building decayed and rooks nested in its rotting roof timbers, Clegg Hall resembled more and more the stereotypical haunted house.

There are two legends relating to the boggarts of Clegg Hall. The founding myth dates back centuries but was expanded by writer G R Oakley in Victorian times: In 1241, Oakley asserted with surprising precision, the drawbridge was lowered at the fortress of the de Cleggs. Henry de Clegg was riding to war in the service of King Henry III who, attempting to wrest Poitou from the French, had summoned all the knights of the realm to his side.

Before galloping away on his white stallion, Henry charged his brother Richard with the care of the hall and his two teenage sons Bertrand and Ranulph. 'Thou couldst not leave them in safer hands,' lied Richard. The brothers embraced and the Baron and his retinue 'turned their steeds toward Rochdale and so to France'.

No sooner had the fleet set sail than Richard began to plot his nephews' demise. Bertrand, the younger brother, trusted his uncle but Ranulph, wiser in the ways of the world, began to suspect Richard's motives.

One dark night Bernard ventured out of the hall alone. Upon his return he climbed the ramparts, failing to notice a shadowy figure stealing up in the dark behind him. But Ranulph de Clegg had spotted his uncle stalking Bertrand.

Richard had chosen his moment well; he could despatch Bertrand with a single thrust of his dagger and push the boy's body into the black waters of the moat.

As Richard was about to strike, Ranulph cried out, 'Brother! Beware!'

Bertrand turned, drawing his own dagger, but Richard was quicker and wheeled around to seize Ranulph by the neck. A single sweep of the blade severed the lad's throat and Richard hurled the body into the water below.

Bertrand gave a cry of anguish and leapt upon the assassin, but Richard was a skilled fighter. He plunged his blade deep into the boy's chest and kicked the dying Bertrand over the parapet to land beside the body of his brother. Richard returned to his room to wash the blood from his tunic and hands.

The English forces had been routed in France and it was a war-weary Henry de Clegg who rode back under the portcullis of Clegg Hall. He was met by Richard, who told his brother of the murder of the two boys by, as he claimed, a stranger's hand. 'I will not rest until I have exacted revenge on the culprit,' swore Richard. But Henry, shattered by his battles and distraught at the fate of his sons, banished his brother for failing in his sacred duty to protect the boys.

*Clegg Hall, home of the boggarts as the* Black Sloven *pub in the 1860s.*
Rochdale Local Studies Library collection

Richard was livid. He had intended to wait until Henry's death by natural causes in order to inherit the hall and its land. Now he had to act. In nearby Stubley Hall lived Hubert de Stubley, who was as steeped in evil as Richard himself. Richard offered the land between Clegg and Stubley to Hubert as reward for his complicity in murdering Henry.

Even though any such passage has still to be discovered, everyone in Rochdale knows that there is a tunnel linking Clegg Hall to Stubley Hall and it was into the gloom of this secret chamber that Richard climbed.

Ignoring the stench, the rats and rotting animal corpses, Richard struggled through the sodden passage until his lantern revealed a white paint daub on a stone wall ahead. He pushed a lever and a panel swung silently open to reveal his brother's bedchamber.

Henry de Clegg lay on the bed grieving for his sons, unable to sleep but unaware of the shadowy figure creeping up behind him.

'Father! Beware!'

Henry leaped to his feet; behind him stood the ghostly figure of his beloved Ranulph and behind Ranulph, his eyes filled with terror at the sight of the child he had so cruelly murdered, was Richard. A dagger dangled from his fingers.

Richard dropped his weapon and ran from the bedchamber, up the stone steps, through the main hall and on to the ramparts. He turned and saw the boy again. With a cry of terror, Richard plunged from the battlements to perish in the icy waters of the moat.

Henry de Clegg owed his life to his murdered son, whose ghost he never saw again.

Plenty of others did though. Nineteenth century folklorist John Roby unearthed (or more probably created) a sequel to the Clegg Hall legend.

According to Roby, in 1662 Alice Howarth and her brother Nicholas lived in the hall. Also in residence was a friar who occupied the 'Boggart Chamber' a room that was still haunted by the restless spirit of Ranulph de Clegg. At a wedding ceremony a series of inexplicable events resulted in the kidnap and disappearance of Alice, the discovery of a hoard of gold, a succession of manifestations of demons and the appearance of 'a legion of devils'. A bull was found, 'perched upon a haystack where he stood as gracefully as a cock on a dunghill'.

The friar was duly revealed as a member of the Clegg family, returned to claim the hall as his rightful inheritance. Suddenly a huge blast shook the building. In the basement, an alchemists' still had exploded. The assembled cast rushed downstairs and there was Alice Howarth released from her imprisonment by the impact of the explosion. All that remained to do was to exorcise the demons.

The fascinating thing about John Roby's flight of fantasy is the implication of 'coining' or forging money by alchemists, at the end of the story. One theory relating to the persistence of the legend of the Clegg Hall Boggart is that the hall had been used as a base for criminal activities and that a good ghost story would deter inquisitive locals. Coiners were undoubtedly operating in the area during this period and it is possible that this element of Roby's tale is based on fact.

The *Rochdale Monthly* of October 1904 recorded what it regarded as the final decline of the building: 'There is now no prospect that the ancient pomp of Clegg Hall will ever be revived. It has deteriorated to the point where it is not capable of being restored.'

Over the next century, the roof caved in, the joists rotted and split and trees grew through the main hall. Then, when everyone had resigned themselves to the structure collapsing, the great-great-great nephew of Robert Kershaw, landlord at Clegg Hall in 1851, proved the *Rochdale Monthly* wrong.

Incredibly, Jason Stead has restored the hall to its former glory. If he encountered any boggarts during the process, he hasn't let on.

CHAPTER 2

# Forging Ahead: Counterfeiters and Coiners

As we saw in the first chapter, it is possible that a gang of forgers used the cellar of Clegg Hall as their base of operations. 'Making false coinage' and forging banknotes was a commonplace if risky activity. Although in the eighteenth century hundreds of crimes on the statute books carried harsh penalties, in practise sentences were often commuted for lesser offences. Being apprehended for, 'undermining the economy by forging the Coin of the Realm', however, meant transportation to Australia, usually for life, or the gallows.

The most notorious gang of coiners in the late eighteenth century operated out of Cragg Vale over the top of Blackstone Edge in Yorkshire. It was an isolated lonely place, a windswept former deer park where the high forests had been sacrificed for shipbuilding and industry.

The local economy mirrored that on the Rochdale side of the border: cottage industries with families supporting their meagre farming income by spinning and weaving wool. Its remoteness made it an ideal location for coining and it was here that David Hartley, 'King David' and his band of forgers, 'clipped the bright guinea'.

Eventually, betrayed by an informer, the gang were involved in the murder of an Excise Officer and hunted down by the Marquis of Rockingham.

The transcript of their trial in 1769 gives a fascinating insight into the methods employed by the forgers: Local innkeepers took genuine gold coins out of circulation and passed them to Hartley. The coins were then sheared, or more commonly clipped, to produce filings of gold. A new milled edge was added to the original coins, which were marginally smaller than before, the change being virtually undetectable. The clippings were then melted down and stamped with engraved dies to replicate the head and tail of the original. The forgeries were then passed back to the publicans who introduced them into circulation.

Hartley and his accomplices were convicted and 'King David' was hung in a blaze of publicity at York on 28 April 1770.

Although counterfeiting coins from gold was the most lucrative process, other metals were regularly used by the forgers. A letter published in the *Gentleman's Magazine* in 1752 revealed that half the copper coins in circulation were fakes and that by substituting metals such as pewter for silver, the coiner could generate a healthy profit. The writer estimated the base metal used by the counterfeiters cost about 8 pence per pound and would yield about 3 shillings in coins. This would give a return of 2 shillings and 4 pence per pound (just over 10 per cent), more than enough to tempt a poor farmer.

To the north of Rochdale, as isolated as, and far more treeless than Cragg Vale, rises Brown Wardle Hill and on the Whitworth side of Brown Wardle is Lobden, a moorland area of stunted grass and rocky outcrops. Here lies the Moonstone, a

*An isolated farm cottage near Wardle.* Rochdale Local Studies Library collection

huge slab of millstone grit said to have been flung from Blackstone Edge by the giant Robin Hood. It was not a place to make a comfortable living by farming, but it was a perfect base for criminal activities.

Farmer, Josiah Shepherd lived in a tiny cottage called *Wall Stones*. In the 1790s he turned to forging silver coins from base metal, sometimes tin, but more usually pewter. When his supply of pewter ran out, Shepherd decided to add theft to his list of crimes by breaking into neighbouring Brown Wardle Farm and stealing the owner's collection of pewter plates. At a stroke, this increased Shepherd's potential profit margin from 10 per cent to 100 per cent.

Unfortunately for him, his finished products had already been detected and the authorities in Rochdale were on the alert for illicit sources of pewter. Knowing that there was a major theft in the Brown Wardle area enabled them to concentrate their resources and an informer provided the police with a name.

Josiah Shepherd was caught in act of counterfeiting a set of half crowns, convicted, and sentenced to transportation for life at Lancaster Assizes. Shepherd was dismayed. He, like many others, considered transportation a fate worse than death.

Originally, the destination for deported prisoners was America, but this option was ended in 1776 with the War of Independence. The alternative, shipping criminals to Australia, made the punishment far harsher. Old rotting warships called 'hulks' transported prisoners to Botany Bay in New South Wales 15,000 miles and 250 days away.

If a prisoner survived the crossing he or she would work in Australia either on public projects or as labourers on private land. The punishment for a variety of misdemeanours was flogging with a 'cat-o'-nine tails' – a whip with nine leather thongs. Serious offences merited 300 lashes.

In the event, Josiah Shepherd was released early but, having spent twenty-one years in irons, returned a broken man. His wife had left the farm to live with a miller in Yorkshire. Shepherd died three years after his return.

Josiah Shepherd's detection was due, not to an effective system of policing, but to a growing network of agent provocateurs, spies and informers established by the government and local business interests.

Increasingly, the informers were co-ordinated by police officers operating on the fringes of the law. The most notorious of these renegade policemen was Joe Naden, or Nadin, constable of Manchester, 'a terrible man with a terrible name' who was used as an agent by the Bank of England.

The Bank of England had first been alerted to the passing of forged notes in Rochdale in May 1803. On the morning of 6 May, brothers Joseph and James Bridge and their friend Thomas Boadle had successfully 'passed a forged 20-shilling note' in the *White Lion Hotel* on Yorkshire Street.

Subsequently the three did the rounds of butchers, bakers and grocers, leaving a trail of forged currency behind them and ending up at the *Cross Keys Inn* for lunch.

Next, the trio visited the *Beaver Inn* where they enjoyed beer and beef steaks. And so to the *Bear*, the *Woolpack* and the *Blue Ball*. Off they went then to Edward Redfearn, butcher, for some mutton chops.

The spree came to an abrupt end when a gaggle of angry tradesmen alerted the Constabulary and the full weight of the law came crashing down on the trio. All three were found guilty of passing false currency at Lancaster Assizes. James Bridge and Thomas Boadle were hung and Joseph Bridge was sentenced to transportation for life.

Bridge's wife was accused of receiving stolen goods but following her reprieve, it was Joseph who alone spent a year on the prison hulk *Phoenix* bound for Australia. There, he petitioned for early release which, after twenty-six years, was granted. It was too late for Joseph Bridge, however, who died in Moreton Bay Australia on 15 February 1829.

Rochdale was clearly a hotbed of coining and forging activity and Constable Joe Naden was contracted by the Bank of England to, 'keep special watch' on the town.

In 1809 a series of near perfect notes on high-quality linen paper produced in Ireland and manufactured in Birmingham, was carried north for distribution. The notes were in denomina-tions of £1, £2 and £5 and represented a small fortune in fraudulent exchange. The plan was to dispose of the bulk of them on market days in Rochdale and several local men were recruited as distributors.

At the foot of Rochdale's 122 Church Steps there is to this day a pub called the *Flying Horse*, which stands on the site of the original hotel of that name. In those days, to the north of the *Flying Horse* were Packer Street and the Gank, where, 'huddled together, were a mass of filthy hovels, foul and noisesome slums, the haunt of prostitutes and felons'. The landlord of the *Flying Horse* in 1809 was James Whitehead, known locally as 'James

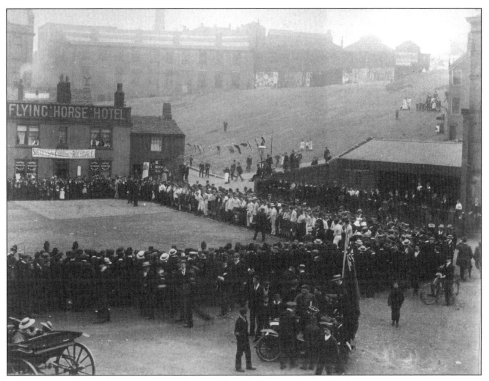

*The* Flying Horse Hotel, *where the Rochdale money launderers were entrapped.*
Rochdale Local Studies Library collection

O'Peter's'.

Constable Joe Naden was familiar with the area. When, exactly a year previously in May 1808 rioters had burnt down Rochdale's gaol, troops and police, Naden amongst them, had been drafted in from Manchester and Halifax and billeted in the town. Naden knew enough about James Whitehead to be confident in using him as a paid agent. Whitehead in his turn approached John Shaw of Smallbridge to assist in the capture of the distributors of the notes.

Joe Naden was working to a precise timetable. He needed arrests on or around 25 July in order that prisoners should stand trial during the August sessions at the Lancaster Assizes. With perfect timing, on the afternoon of 25 July, Gilbert Holden, a labourer from Intack Cottage near Whitworth, walked into the *Flying Horse*.

James Whitehead and John Shaw suspected Holden of being one of the major dealers in forged notes, so Whitehead approached Holden asking if he could supply him with counterfeit currency. Holden replied that he 'had none about his person'. However he returned later in the evening with three fake notes for which Whitehead paid, 'a percentage of their face value'.

Holden returned to his cottage to be rudely awakened that night as John Naden and six constables battered down his door and arrested him. Also captured, thanks to evidence provided by James Whitehead and John Shaw, were: James Cudworth, farmer, of Meadowhead, Lawrence Law, labourer, of Millgate and James Draper a farmer from Whitworth.

The Hue and Cry (Naden was not subtle) alerted the last of the suspects, Thomas Howarth of Hades near Wardle. Howarth fled across the moors and hid for three weeks in the rushes alongside the ancient track known as the Long Causeway. He was brought food and blankets by relatives and finally escaped into Yorkshire. Remarkably he was never captured and managed eventually to return home.

The others were not so fortunate. At the Lancaster Assizes on 14 August 1809 Holden, Law, Cudworth and Draper were each accused of, 'uttering forged banknotes'. Draper, charged

*The open moorland around Rochdale provided the perfect location for forgers and coiners.* Rochdale Local Studies Library collection

with issuing twenty-five notes was identified as the ringleader.

Holden's defence counsel, Solomon Yates of Lancaster launched a robust rebuttal on his behalf, accusing Whitehead and Shaw of entrapment. 'The policy of the law in England,' he argued, 'is not to procure the commission of a crime for the purpose of inflicting a punishment, but rather to prevent its perpetration.'

Nevertheless, the jury found all four guilty as charged and they were duly sentenced to death. The judge, however, was troubled by the notion that Holden had been entrapped and ordered a respite in the proceedings until 24 November in order that he could consult with his fellow judges on the point of law.

Solomon Yates was given a second opportunity to present his legal argument. On 11 November he delivered a detailed address to three judges in the Executive Chamber, citing James Whitehead, John Shaw and Constable Joe Naden for entrapment. Despite Yates' efforts, the original verdict of the jury and the sentences of the judge at Lancaster were upheld. However, Joe Naden's methods were being questioned at last.

The families of the condemned men, including Holden's elderly father, travelled to Lancaster to witness the execution, which took place on the night of 24 November. Gilbert Holden's body was placed in a coffin and given to his father to transport back to Rochdale. The hangman's noose was deliberately left around the corpse's neck.

Public sympathy was with the felons and when Holden's body arrived back in Whitworth, it was buried in consecrated ground at Hallfold Chapel. The tombstone bore simply his name, date of death and his age, twenty-seven.

James Whitehead was paid well for his work and bought three cottages in Milnrow with the proceeds. Whitehead was widely ostracised and for years locals referred to his Milnrow terrace as 'Hangman's Row'.

John Shaw's conscience plagued him. His contemporaries accused him of taking 'blood money' and to appease them he bought bags of grain to distribute free to the poor and needy in Rochdale market. So few accepted his gift that 'he was obliged to take it home and feed his pigs with it'.

Joe Naden continued to recruit to his network of spies and informers. In 1815 three Irishmen newly arrived in Manchester were approached by one of Naden's agents who possessed a store of counterfeit coins. The agent offered cash to the trio for polishing the forgeries 'to a fine lustre' and then reported them to Naden for the 'blood money' reward. The three were arrested but appealed to their local priest who informed the magistrates of Naden's involvement. All three accused received free pardons and the practise of offering blood money was officially abandoned. Naden's credibility and reputation went with it.

Constable Joe Naden was forced into retirement and spent his later years farming in Cheshire. No longer the force he had been in his younger days, Naden's farm was a constant target for thieves. 'They visited him more frequently than they did any other farmer and stole his horses and poultry with impunity.'

Even in his prime, Naden had one Rochdale-based nemesis who consistently eluded him. Peter Wilson was an enterprising crook who posed as a respectable middleman in the Rochdale woollen trade, 'his headquarters in a lock-up shop next to the *Bishop Blaize*; the weavers' meeting place in Rochdale Market'.

Here Wilson received stolen goods by the cartload and passed off forged banknotes. Under the shop, 'was a cellar where his plunder was hidden and from whence a pulley device

*False currency was passed in pubs and at events such as the local bull bait.*
Rochdale Local Studies Library collection

conveyed forged currency up to his serving area'.

For years Constable John Naden pursued Pete Wilson, resorting on more than one occasion to bribery and his network of spies and informers. All to no avail; Wilson's façade of respectability was unshakeable.

Wilson and others like him in Rochdale were able to thrive because, in spite of the activities of spies and agents, crime was out of control. This was partially an effect of the town's rapidly increasing population, but was mostly due to ineffective administrative systems.

Eventually, aware that the town was ungovernable and fast becoming a haven for criminal elements, a handful of wealthy manufacturers applied to the Government for policing powers. The subsequent Rochdale Police Act, passed in 1825, directed that the town should be managed by 'Commissioners of Police' who would operate like a Town Council.

The day-to-day 'policing' of Rochdale was to be carried out by 'able-bodied watchmen, night patrol and beadles'. The Act also authorized, 'the appointment of a Chief Constable to oversee the Constabulary'.

Crooked businessman Peter Wilson, encouraged by his success in Rochdale, decided to try his luck in a bigger arena. At about the time of the establishment of the Rochdale Police Commission, Wilson moved to Manchester. He opened a 'general store' on Shudehill market and continued his undercover career as fence and money launderer.

However, although he had been able to run rings around Constable John Naden, Peter Wilson was about to meet his match. Charles Johnson was Chief-Constable of Chorlton-on-Medllock, one of the poorest and most unruly areas of Manchester. Like Naden before him, Johnson was not above setting up a 'sting' to catch his prey.

He ordered one of his officers to pose as a burglar and approach Wilson to act as a fence for stolen gold plate and jewellery. Wilson fell for the ruse and Johnson himself performed the arrest.

Charles Johnson's satisfaction, however, was tempered by the fact that 'Wilson received a trifling sentence of only two year's imprisonment'. The adversaries would meet again.

In 1829 rioting had broken out in Rochdale. Although the Police Commissioners had possessed the authority to appoint a chief police officer for four years, 'they had hesitated until a suitable candidate could be found'. The Tories on Rochdale's magisterial bench were so impressed with the methods of

Charles Johnson they offered him the post of Chief Constable. Johnson accepted the offer and took office immediately.

Meanwhile, Peter Wilson had been released and re-established himself as a money launderer in Yorkshire. Here he worked with an accomplice called Aaron Dawson. Wilson was soon apprehended passing forged notes in a public house but turned King's evidence. Dawson was transported for fourteen years and Wilson sped out of Yorkshire back to Rochdale, disguised as Church of England clergyman.

One afternoon, Chief Constable Charles Johnson, strolling up Yorkshire Street, passed a vicar going in the opposite direction. Both men did a double take. Johnson turned on his heels, overtook the cleric and stared at his face. There was mutual recognition. The two men nodded to each other and went their separate ways.

Johnson returned to the Police Commission Rooms at the top of Yorkshire Street and called three 'runners' into his office. He instructed them not to let Peter Wilson out of their sight and to report any suspicious behaviour back to Johnson. Wilson, aware that he was being shadowed, left Rochdale for Yorkshire where, within a week, he and an accomplice were arrested for passing forged notes.

Again Wilson tried to turn King's Evidence but this time the Bank of England was not interested. In a desperate attempt to secure a reprieve from the death sentence, Wilson asked to be returned to the custody of his nemesis Charles Johnson. The court agreed and Wilson returned to Rochdale in chains. He led Charles Johnson to Folly Field off Whitworth Road. There, Wilson pulled a tin box out of a dry sewer and handed it to Johnson. Inside was over £500 in counterfeit Bank of England notes, a fortune.

In the event, the court commuted Wilson's death sentence. He was transported for life.

Although forgery and passing fake currency remain commonplace to this day, it became increasingly difficult to establish bases for these activities in the Pennine hills. Policing methods gradually improved and there were more officers to keep an eye on isolated farms and homesteads. The days of the Rochdale coiners were over.

# CHAPTER 3

# Highway Robbery!

This is a story of highwaymen, possible mistaken identity, amateur detection and political intrigue. It begins in 1835 with a race meeting and ends in the following year with a hanging and it involves warring factions from every social class in Rochdale.

Members of established Rochdale families behaved like lords and ladies of the manor, demanding deference and respect from those further down the social scale. Of these wealthy local dynasties, no family wielded more power than the Royds.

The founder of the line, John Royds of Marled Earth, Wardle had been a cloth-maker, exporting his finished products to Holland, Spain and Portugal. He passed his fortune down to his son James who expanded into wholesale merchanting.

By 1827, the then head of the family, Clement Royds was able to move into banking, overseeing the largest financial institution in the Parish of Rochdale. He was also a magistrate. It was said that when Royds raised the drooping eyelid covering his blind right eye, the accused could expect a lengthy sentence.

Clement Royds had two sons, William Edward and Albert Hudson and it was the latter that turned out to be a 'chip off the old block'. Albert, born in 1811, quickly acquired a taste for all things military. Not that he ever went to war. The closest Albert Hudson Royds ever got to a skirmish was as Commander-in-Chief of the faintly ludicrous Rochdale Yeomanry, a volunteer force mercilessly lampooned by the local press for engaging in mock battles on Cronkeyshaw Common.

At the time of the events described here, Albert Hudson Royds was twenty-four years of age.

The romantic image of Highway Robbery carried out by Dick Turpin look-alikes on jet-black mares shouting, 'Stand and Deliver!' was an eighteenth-century invention. The reality was far more mundane. Highwaymen were usually footpads tramping the muddy thoroughfares and most attacks were

*A Royds Bank £5 note.* Rochdale Local Studies Library collection

violent and poorly executed. The practise did not disappear with the eighteenth century. In the 1830s unlit rural roads provided numerous opportunities for highway robbery.

There is an area between Rochdale and Middleton called Slattocks. The Rochdale Canal was dug through here in 1801, the engineers taking advantage of the unusual flatness of the terrain. The land to the north of the old turnpike road then rises gradually through the hamlet of Thornham to Tandle Hill. The countryside itself is low-lying, with a continuation of the sparse vegetation and murky rivulets that typify Castleton Moor. Rough bushes and hedgerows are scattered throughout and there is the occasional copse providing both shelter and a hiding place. Then as now, there were few houses, just a pub and a handful of isolated farms and cottages. At night the place was dark and as quiet as the grave, allowing poachers to ply their trade undisturbed. The area was outside the normal sphere of influence of the Royds family, being nearer to Middleton than Rochdale.

Riders bound for Manchester and Rochdale passed through Slattocks and the 1830s saw a marked increase in incidents of robbery in the area. Highway robbers paid no heed to class or social standing, the wealthier the potential victim the better. In March 1835, John Taylor, one of the Whitworth Doctors, celebrated for their treatment of Queen Charlotte, was attacked and robbed, to enormous public outrage. He was one of seven victims of highwaymen in a period of three months.

A series of arrests were made in April 1835 and Thomas Eastwood, a local man, was tried and convicted. Eastwood, however, had powerful friends in Middleton including Captain Hopwood of nearby Hopwood Hall. On 3 June 1835, the *Manchester Guardian* reported that 'Thomas Eastwood has been released through the instrumentality of Captain Hopwood and the testimony of several respectable persons that Eastwood was 2 miles away from the place at the time the robbery was committed.' The Home Secretary, Lord John Russell, had granted Eastwood a free pardon.

The pardon infuriated the police and magistrates but it didn't take long, following his release, for Eastwood to find himself in trouble again.

Albert Hudson Royds, his brother, William Edward Royds and their servant, Benjamin Galtress, arrived on horseback at Brick Field between Slattocks and Trub Smithy at about 11.15pm on Thursday 24 September 1835, having spent a day at the Heaton Park races.

The riders discovered that the road through Slattocks was blocked so, as it was, according to Albert Royds' subsequent statement, a 'starlit night with good visibility' the three took to the footpath. As they passed the Brick Field, Albert Royds realizing that this was where the assault on the Whitworth Doctor had taken place, turned to his brother and said: 'This is the very spot where those scoundrels . . .' Right on cue, he received a sharp crack on the side of his head. He slumped forward in his saddle, taking three more heavy blows as a number of men grabbed his reins. His dug in his spurs and his horse bolted, carrying him to safety.

However, the sound of a scuffle and a series of loud groans told him his brother was in trouble. Albert judiciously hid his gold watch into his boot before charging to the rescue. William was on the ground with several bodies on top of him. Albert's yeomanry training held him in good stead. 'I pressed both heels to my horse's sides and made a charge at those men,' he said later. 'My horse plunged and fought at them very savagely with his forefeet.' Royds thought that the horse's hooves had made contact with one or more of the attackers but couldn't be sure.

The men kept raining blows on the Royds brothers; one attacker, later identified by Albert as John Elson of Slattocks, grabbing hold of the horse's bridle, pulling him to a halt. Albert, nearly unseated by his assailants, offered them money, passing over 5 shillings to a man he later swore to be the recently pardoned Thomas Eastwood. A third man, who Royds identified as Sidney Kay and who was obviously wise to old 'hiding-the watch-in the-boot routine', pulled off Albert's boot and sock and pocketed the watch. One of the assailants allegedly shouted, 'Hast thou got it?' and lunged at Royds with a pole. 'Three men then ran off across the Brick Field.'

William Royds had been badly beaten. Albert half-dragged and half-carried him to the turnpike house at Trub Smithy and rode into Rochdale to alert the Chief Constable. Slattocks was strictly speaking outside the jurisdiction of the Rochdale Force but that would not have bothered Albert Hudson Royds. Nor would it have troubled Rochdale's Chief Constable, Charles Johnson.

Johnson, who was a political appointee supported by Clement Royds and the Tories on the Rochdale Police Commission, had proved an unpopular choice. Complaints against him were constant. In 1831 a motion in front of the Police Commission to dismiss him was only narrowly defeated. The following month he was ordered to lay down a bond of £300, forfeited if he failed to carry out his duties effectively.

Johnson exercised virtually no control over his watchmen and beadles who were regularly sacked by the Watch Committee for neglect of duty, misconduct and assault. Typically, James Taylor, a constable who was jailed for two years for stealing money from the Weavers' Union cashbox, was reinstated as Constable for the Township of Spotland immediately following his release.

Despite all this, Charles Johnson continued to be supported by the Royds, if only because he was their appointee. However, when Albert Royds went that night to the house of the Chief Constable he found Johnson to be, 'indisposed'. The Watch Committee had already noted how fragile their Chief Constable's health was.

Johnson's two sons, Francis and Peter were drafted in to investigate the robbery, although they had no authority whatsoever to carry out police investigations. Peter was later to become a leading figure in the town but now he was barely eighteen years old. Nevertheless, he was instructed by his ailing father to accompany Albert Hudson Royds to the scene of the crime.

Near a break in the hedgerow at Brick Field the pair met two passers-by who had just found the sock and boot taken from Albert Royds by his attackers. Encouraged by this, Royds and Johnson began scouring the area.

In March 2007, the UK Forensic Science Service launched

*Albert Hudson Royds – target of the Slattocks Highwaymen.*
Rochdale Local Studies Library collection

the world's first database of shoe-prints from crime scenes. 'Shoe marks,' the accompanying report noted, 'are still the second most common type of identification evidence after DNA.' The investigative techniques of Peter Johnson and Albert Hudson pre-dated the report by 200 years.

The pair identified a unique series of footprints in the mud ('during repair each shoe had lost a nail from the toe'), following the trail in a semi-circle to the north corner of Brick Field where they were joined by Francis Johnson and two constables.

The meandering course taken by the five sleuths ended at the cottage of Sidney Kay. Kay, arriving home some ten minutes later, spotted Peter Johnson and Constable William Taylor and turned to flee. Johnson called him back, confiscated the hare Kay had just poached and marched him to the *Slattocks Inn*, along with a pair of his boots. There, the boots were compared to a mould made of the footprints and found to be a match. Pressed into the ground beside the footprints themselves, the boots made an identical indentation.

Sidney Kay was taken into custody to the lock-up in Rochdale, 'where his hat was removed and he was discovered to have a wound on his head that was bleeding profusely'.

John Elson was arrested merely for having been seen in the company of Sidney Kay at around the time of the robbery. Thomas Eastwood was picked up as the result of equally cir-cumstantial evidence, but all three were positively identified by Albert Hudson Royds when he visited them later that day in Rochdale's lock-up. Two other suspects who were questioned were subsequently released, but not before a revealing conver-sation had allegedly taken place between all five men in the cells.

All that was necessary to make an escape from the gaol in Rochdale was to open an unlocked door, descend six stone steps into a small courtyard, climb the corresponding steps at the other side and jump over an iron gate to freedom. A number of suspects did this only to return voluntarily in time for their committal.

Charles Johnson (back on his feet following his indisposi-tion), ordered Constable James Taylor of weavers' cash box fame to spy on the five prisoners and prevent their escape. Taylor claimed later to have overheard a conversation between the suspects that implicated Kay, Elson and Eastwood in the felony but he (Taylor) was not considered a reliable enough witness to give evidence at the subsequent hearing.

*The Lockup on Rope Street – Rochdale's insecure gaol.*
Rochdale Local Studies Library collection

The trial took place in January 1836 at Liverpool Assizes. It emerged that Charles Johnson, who had arrested Eastwood on his previous robbery charge and was incensed at his subsequent pardon, had tried to persuade Sidney Kay to turn King's Evidence against Eastwood. The attempt had failed on a legal technicality.

Meanwhile, the press were implying that Clement Royds, a close friend of one of the magistrates at Eastwood's original trial, was seeking retribution on behalf of his colleague and had been lobbying the government to ensure that the prisoner did not walk free again. There was also a distinct ground swell of opinion amongst Middleton residents that Rochdale magistrates were meddling affairs that did not concern them.

The *Manchester Guardian* even claimed: 'It was common knowledge that the night of the attack, far from being starlit, was far too gloomy for Mr Royds to have identified his attackers.'

Back in court, much was made by the prosecution of the evidence of the footprints in the mud and the fact that Kay was bleeding from his head when he was arrested, allegedly as a result of being struck by the hooves of Albert Hudson Royds' horse.

The footprints were explained by the defence by asserting that yes; those had been Kay's boot-marks, but that he was a poacher not a highwayman. As to the wound on Kay's head, his brother Thomas claimed: 'My brother was in a quarrel which led to a fight; he had a wound on his head and a black eye.' James Barrow, landlord of a public house on Bridge Street, confirmed that the fight had taken place stating: 'Sidney Kay fell in a scuffle on my premises and bruised his head on a fender.'

*Sidney Kay claimed to have received his head injury in a Middleton pub.*
Rochdale Local Studies Library collection

There were, however, a number of witnesses claiming to have seen either two, or all three, of the accused together at potentially incriminating times during the night.

The trio were found guilty, sentenced to transportation for life and taken to the holding cells at Chatham Docks.

Then, totally out of the blue, three Irish highwaymen confessed to the attack on the Royds brothers at Slattocks and a campaign was launched calling for the immediate pardon and release of Kay, Eastwood and Elson.

The Irishmen had been arrested in March 1836 following a series of robberies, for which they were swiftly tried, convicted and sentenced to death. Having been condemned to hang, they were visited by a priest who would grant them absolution only if they confessed to any unsolved crimes that they had committed. Amongst thirty unresolved offences, the three admitted to the highway robbery of the, 'young gentlemen near Manchester in September 1835'.

The trio from Slattocks were awaiting transportation at Chatham when the news of the confession broke. They remained in the dockyard cells until the Irishmen's statements could be taken in Shrewsbury where they were awaiting execution.

Captain Hopwood organized the lobbying on behalf of Eastwood and the others, sending a petition for pardon, 'signed by over four hundred people' to the Home Secretary.

The Royds acted quickly to nip this deteriorating situation in the bud. Clement and Albert Hudson Royds, Chief Constable Charles Johnson, the prosecution attorney for the case, William Taylor and his clerk, travelled to Shrewsbury, as they said without a hint of irony, 'to ensure that no external pressure was put on the prisoners or the authorities at the gaol'.

The document, which worried the Royds' contingent, was a transcription of a statement by Patrick McDaniel, the eldest of the three brothers in custody.

> **Who committed the robbery?** . . . *Myself and my two brothers Edward and Owen and four others.* **How was the attack made?** . . . *Three persons were coming up on horseback. One was smoking a cigar. One of them observed, 'this is where the vagabonds robbed . . .' I stopped them and searched one of the persons and found a watch concealed in his boot.*

McDaniel went on to describe how he took a few shillings from Albert Hudson Royds and fenced the watch in Liverpool.

Clement and Albert Hudson Royds were advised against questioning the prisoners in person and remained in their hotel on the outskirts of the town. However, in the gaol, the process to which the Irishmen were subjected resembled a court hearing. William Taylor interrogated each separately and Charles Johnson, 'suggested questions to be put when their statements were at variance with the facts as he knew them to be

Two of the brothers were questioned at length. Both claimed to be part of a larger gang although each was either reluctant or unable to provide the names of their accomplices.

William Taylor's clerk took copious notes, which Taylor transcribed. In the transcript, Taylor maintained that there were too many discrepancies in the three statements to make the Irishmen's confession plausible. He theorized that on the slender chance of a commutation of the death sentence, the Irishmen had cobbled together a confession out of second and third-hand accounts of the crime.

There certainly are discrepancies in their statements, including contradictions as to the alleged time of the attack, confusion over the route taken by the attackers and disagreement with the Royds' version as to method of the assault. However, the evidence seems hardly conclusive either way. The Irishmen were able to give far more than a broad outline of the incident and were hardly likely to have been scouring the newspapers for reports of robberies on the off-chance of confessing to a crime that they did not commit.

Much was made by William Taylor of Albert Hudson Royds hearing one of his attackers shout in relation to his watch: 'Hast thou got it?' and that this was not an Irish but a northern English mode of speech. So it was, but all the condemned Irishmen claimed to have had two or three companions of unknown nationality with them that night.

And there is one particularly intriguing extract in the Irishmen's statement. Two of the three claimed that Albert Hudson Royds cried out to his attackers not to hurt his brother because he was 'delicate not firm'. This infirmity was not mentioned by Royds in his testimony or in the newspaper accounts; yet William Edward Royds was not considered robust and significantly played no part in the arrest, the court case, or its aftermath.

The press was incensed at the interference of the Royds and their supporters but in the end it was up to the Home Secretary, Lord John Russell, to decide whether to pardon Thomas Eastwood (for a second time) and his companions. This he declined to do. To be seen pardoning the same man for the same offence twice in twelve months would not have been good politics. Accordingly, to the jubilation of the Royds and their followers, Lord John Russell issued a statement that the petition for the pardoning of Kay, Eastwood and Elson was denied.

The trio from Slattocks were transported to Australia for life in October 1836. A month later the three Irishmen were hung in Shrewsbury gaol.

*Willaim Edward Royds . . . 'not considered robust'.*
Rochdale Local Studies Library collection

# CHAPTER 4

# The Half-Moon Horror

**B**y the 1850s, the wealthy mill-owners and merchants who had originally made their homes near the centre of Rochdale had moved to the outskirts of the town, building huge walled mansions with wrought iron gates to deter unwanted visitors. The town itself was the home of the workers, living near to the factories in terraces and courtyards. The 'golden age' of terrace living when, 'everyone knew their neighbour and folk looked out for one another', was in the future.

In 1855, Rochdale was a dark forbidding place, a filthy river, stained with dye, divided the town into two sections: poor and poorer.

On the north of the river were Yorkshire Street and the market. Blackwater Street partially paved with slippery stone setts veered away from Lord Street at a ninety degree angle towards St Mary's Gate. As it narrowed past the *Bishop Blaize* and *Duke of Wellington* inns, Blackwater Street consisted of clusters of stone-built hovels and decaying tenements with steps down to dingy, airless cellar dwellings. Here, by the lane to Brickcoft, the passage was no more than 5 feet wide and at the top was Half-Moon Yard and the *Half-Moon Inn*.

Most people who stayed in the crumbling cottages of Half-Moon Yard were itinerants, labourers and their families travelling to wherever work could be found and moving on. In the main, they were invisible, unmemorable and unknown. The *Half-Moon Inn* was a three-storey ruin, a maze of ill-lit corridors with narrow stairways and tiny foul-smelling rooms. On the ground floor was the low ceilinged taproom, bedecked with flickering oil-lamps, which burned day and night. Here a room could be rented with no questions asked, although the ill-assorted couples that did so got little in the way of privacy.

On Saturday 21 July 1855, a man went into the taproom of the *Half-Moon Inn* and asked the landlady, Elizabeth Asquith,

*Half-Moon Yard – residents were itinerant labourers, 'unmemorable and unknown'.*
Rochdale Local Studies Library collection

for a room for himself and his wife. He paid the 8 pence tariff in advance, left the pub and returned with a woman. The two sat quietly in a corner for about half an hour, occasionally talking but not in a particularly animated way. 'Indeed,' as the landlord stated later, 'there seemed to be some quiet animosity between them.' At eleven o'clock the man asked if the landlady's daughter could take them to their room. In the event it was Mrs Asquith who showed them the way, saying, 'they could lock the door if they so wished'.

Nothing was heard from the room during the night and at six o'clock the next morning the man came down the stairs alone, followed by the landlady's son, Edmund Ashworth. The man opened the back door only to find that it led into a courtyard bounded by a high stone wall. He appeared to be contemplating scaling the wall when Edmund Asquith offered to unlock the gate. As he hurried through the gateway, the man turned to Asquith, saying he would be back in half an hour or so.

By midday there was no sign of him. The landlord sent a female servant upstairs to investigate. As she half opened the door to the room, the girl stopped. She had seen splashes of what looked like blood on the floor. She slammed the door shut and went hurriedly downstairs, bumping into Edmund Asquith who then ran to the room himself. He flung the door open.

A terrible sight greeted him. The woman was lying across the bed, her throat cut from ear to ear. The bedclothes were saturated with blood and more blood had congealed on the floor. A pillow had been placed against the woman's throat and was resting by her shoulder. The underside was sodden with blood. It was a scene of total carnage

Edmund plunged down the narrow stairs, 'his shouts resembling screams'. Landlord Stephen Asquith sent a servant to fetch the police before he had even gone upstairs to check the body.

Rochdale Borough Constabulary was no longer the laughing stock it had been. Superintendent Jervis, Sergeant Leach and three constables arrived, running pell-mell from the nearby police offices. Jervis set up an interview area in the taproom of the pub where he interrogated the Asquith's, two boarders, neighbours and the drinkers from the previous night. He didn't have much to go on. Nobody knew the couple.

What Jervis did manage to piece together was a detailed description of the man. He was about fifty years of age, 5 foot 8 inches tall, with dark, greying hair and wearing a black topcoat with tears in the elbow, a light-coloured smock and black cord trousers. The description of clothing was of vital importance in those days. Poorer people seldom had more than one set of clothes, which they would constantly repair and occasionally wash. Identification was as often achieved via outer garments as physical characteristics.

Based on the witness accounts, the police were convinced that the suspect was an itinerant labourer or a stonemason. It was therefore a source of great satisfaction in the Rochdale Police Offices when, armed with the description provided by Superintendent Jervis, a Constable Brown arrested a man travelling from Blackburn to Preston that very afternoon.

An estimated ten thousand curious onlookers crammed into the narrow streets as the prisoner, William Martin, was led in chains through the town to the lock-ups. The events were proving a sensation, regionally as well as locally. It was the first suspected murder in Rochdale in over thirty years, although, significantly, it would not be thirty years until another was committed. The press turned out in force; the *Rochdale Sentinel, Manchester Guardian, Manchester Courier* and *Manchester Examiner* each despatched two or more reporters to cover the inquest, which took place in the *Half-Moon Inn* on Tuesday 24 July. The prisoner Martin stood chained, surrounded by four constables.

A pin could have been heard dropping in the packed taproom as the first witness, surgeon Joseph Seed gave his evidence.

> *The woman was lying on the bed. Her hair, pillows and the bed were soaked with blood, a channel of which marked the wall and a pool of blood was lodged on the floor below. The right hand was holding in its grasp a razor, the back of its haft towards the face. The razor had not the least speck of blood upon it and neither was it fairly grasped. The woman seemed about forty-five years of age, of masculine appearance, a profusion of dark grey hair, grey eyes, high cheekbones, snubbed nose, relaxed mouth and a gap in her front upper teeth.*
>
> *There was a deep wound about six inches in length across her throat, the upper and gristly part of the windpipe completely divided, its lower orifice protruding and filled with frothy mucus, three muscles completely cut through. The aspect of her face did not suggest a struggle but there was blood in her stomach caused, I think by the swallowing of blood following an attempt at suffocation with a pillow.*

The Coroner asked Dr Seed whether the razor had been placed in the hand of the deceased after her death, which he replied was 'highly likely'.

Edmund Asquith was called and stated that he had identified the prisoner William Martin out of three men present in the lock-up. Martin, exercising his right to question the witness, first asked if the man who had rented the room on the night of the murder had drunk much and whether the witness had seen him (Martin) in Rochdale before. Receiving a negative answer to both questions, Martin then became fixated as to the colour of the suspect's hair. He asked three consecutive witnesses: 'Did you not say the man had dark hair?' All three denied having described the hair as being dark, although at least two had in fact done so when interviewed by the police. Martin appears to have given up at this point, 'standing with shoulders slumped and a hopeless air about him'.

One female witness described how 'the prisoner and a woman had tried to find lodgings with me in Griffin Yard'. The Coroner had Martin turn around and asked the woman if she could identify him. 'His hair looks lighter now,' she replied, 'it was dark.' Martin said nothing.

Finally Sergeant Leach incurred the wrath of the Coroner by 'muttering his evidence so hardly a word could be understood'. He showed the jury the clothes worn by the deceased. 'She wore,' he mumbled, 'a lilac dress with small white patterns, a red and green shawl of cashmere a blue neckerchief and a straw bonnet.' Nothing on the body or in the clothing could help to identify the victim. However, Leach concluded, 'it was clear that the woman was respectable because of the cleanliness of her underthings.'

Four witnesses identified William Martin as the man in the *Half-Moon Inn* and the prisoner gave a garbled account of his whereabouts on the Saturday night, eventually claiming, to nobody's satisfaction, that he was in Blackburn. Martin was then taken from the inn and remanded in custody.

Superintendent Jervis was concerned that the police knew as little about William Martin as they did about the murdered woman. Learning that he had a brother, Richard, in Middlesbrough, Jervis despatched a constable to bring Richard Martin to Rochdale and formally identify the prisoner.

Richard Martin was busy; he acknowledged that he had a brother who had been working in the Rochdale area but said that his name was Christopher, not William. He also had a second brother, James, who would, said Richard Martin, accompany the constable to Rochdale.

The following morning James Martin, 'a huge, red-faced man', entered the prisoner's cell with Superintendent Jervis. 'Do you recognize this man?' Jervis asked William Martin. 'Yes,' replied the prisoner, 'it is my brother.' 'I do not recognize you sir!' shouted James Martin, lunging past Superintendent Jervis and attempting to kick and punch the prisoner. It took Jervis and three constables to restrain James Martin and bundle him out of the cell. 'I don't know this man!' bellowed James Martin. He stormed out of the lock-up to the railway station and caught a train back to Middlesbrough.

The body of the victim had still not been identified and consequently had not been buried. The weather was getting hotter and Dr Seed was of the opinion that 'it would not keep much longer'. The victim was buried, on Wednesday 25 July with no mourners in attendance.

Meanwhile, the press coverage had reached fever pitch with reporters now arriving from Preston and Blackburn as well as Manchester. On the same day as the burial, the first reports of the inquest appeared in the Manchester press. A Peter Mayers from Salford read the transcripts and, from the description of the clothing, was confident that he recognized both the victim and the suspect. The woman, he said, had lodged with him during the previous year and the man had been a regular visitor.

Mayers travelled to Rochdale and positively identified the clothing of the deceased as belonging to Margaret Jones, his former lodger. Peter Mayers was certain he would recognize her companion but when he went to the lock-ups was astonished to be confronted by a total stranger.

Shortly after Mayer's arrival in Rochdale, three brothers from Manchester stepped off a train and asked the station master their way to the Rochdale Police Offices. They were, they said, all sons of Margaret Jones who they believed had been murdered in the town by a man called Jonathan Heywood. Once at the police station, they repeated their story to Superintendent Jervis and positively identified the clothing of the victim as belonging to their mother, Margaret Jones.

Jervis then had the unenviable task of organizing the disinterment of the body for the purposes of final identification. 'Considerable decomposition had taken place' but the brothers recognized their mother and at last the victim had a name and someone to mourn her. The three brothers were also able to give a detailed background of the new suspect, Jonathan Heywood.

Heywood, they said, had been born in Spotland outside Rochdale in or around 1800, to poor parents. His mother died when he was six, leaving his father with little choice but to send Jonathan and his eight brothers and sisters out to work. Eventually he moved into Rochdale, finding employment as a handloom weaver in Wardleworth. Here he met his first wife Sarah Butterworth from the Paddock area of the town. The couple had three children and went to live in Manchester in the early 1830s. Sarah Butterworth, a deeply religious woman, died in 1848 and soon afterwards John Heywood abandoned his voluntary work at the local Methodist Sunday School and started drinking heavily.

Heywood began seeing Margaret Jones in 1851. The opinion of her family was that he was a 'worthless character'; the brothers seemed particularly hostile, to the point of threatening Heywood with violence every time they encountered him. For a time, Heywood and Margaret Jones lived together, causing the youngest of the brothers, Tom, to leave home.

There was talk of marriage, usually by Margaret Jones, who eventually threw Heywood out, 'as living in sin was not what she had in mind'. Heywood pursued her, however and the two would still meet, usually clandestinely and never when the children were in the house. Heywood would stay overnight, leaving at five or six in the morning.

In June 1855, Heywood began pestering Margaret Jones to marry him. The venue always had to be Rochdale.

A Charlotte Albinson from Manchester then came forward to confirm the brothers' statement and to add that Margaret Jones had left Manchester for Rochdale, believing that she was to be married to Jonathan Heywood on Saturday 23 July. Superintendent Jervis climbed the 122 steps to the Parish Church of St Chad to consult their records. There were no banns of marriage posted for a Jonathan Heywood and a Margaret Jones.

So the police had a second suspect, but where was he? If the murderer was Heywood, not Martin then no one had reported seeing him since he walked out of the gate of the *Half-Moon Inn* on that fateful Sunday morning.

Such was the level of publicity generated by the case that scores of people came forward with information. Heywood, it transpired, had a brother on Gibson Row, Rochdale with whom he had been living for the last three weeks. Superintendent Jervis interviewed the brother at his home and found out that this was where Heywood went after he had left the *Half-Moon Inn*. He had changed his hat and overcoat, telling his brother he was leaving to get job haymaking at Widdup's Farm, next to the Cemetery. This was a long hot walk up Bury Road, but when Jervis arrived he discovered that Heywood had not been seen at the farm.

Two days later, Jervis interviewed a labourer who reported that he had seen someone answering Jonathan Heywood's description making their way to Buckley's Farm, north of Whitworth.

Superintendent Jervis drove to Buckley's Farm and questioned an Irishman who confirmed that Heywood had worked there and had taken great interest in the newspaper accounts of the inquest. When the Irishman had said he thought William Martin would hang, Heywood replied simply: 'No he won't.'

On the day before Jervis' arrival at Buckley Farm, Heywood had stolen food from his workmates and left without collecting his wages. Jervis and his constables spent the next two days distributing 'wanted' notices and on Friday 3 August Heywood, carrying a bundle of rushes, was finally arrested by Constable Andrew Barry, a plain-clothes officer, at Coupe outside Whitworth.

*Scene of the murder – the* Half-Moon Inn. Rochdale Local Studies Library collection

Barry, with Heywood in handcuffs beside him, walked the 6 miles to Rochdale, to the entertainment of the passers-by. Heywood, 'who strode with his head erect, happily made indecent remarks to the females who spoke to him along the road'.

On the following Thursday, the adjourned inquest was resumed at the *Half-Moon Inn*.

Much to their frustration, the press were excluded from the first session, the Coroner being of the opinion that too many details relating to the suspects had been made public. This action was considered particularly unfair by the gentlemen of the press, as it had been the level of publicity generated by them which had alerted the witnesses from Manchester, resulting in the identification of both the victim and the suspect.

At this point there were still two prisoners in the lock-up. To the confusion of the jury, William Martin, who was brought to the hearing together with Heywood, introduced himself as 'Christopher Martin'.

Heywood smiled throughout the proceedings. Martin looked dejected, but a series of witnesses now confidently stated that Heywood not Martin was the man they had seen at the *Half-Moon Inn*. The family of Margaret Jones all agreed that they could see some resemblance between the two men, but that Martin's hair was far greyer and that he had bushier side-whiskers.

Jonathan Heywood chose to question only Martin, which he did, to no significant purpose, and then claimed to have been staying with a former girlfriend on the night of the murder.

However, the most revealing testimony came from Charlotte Albinson. She had lodged with Margaret Jones and had loaned her an umbrella and gloves for the supposed wedding. Albinson stated that Joseph Heywood had been attempting to meet Jones in Rochdale for three consecutive Saturdays. When she had not turned up on the first two occasions, Heywood had been furious, saying, 'he had incurred the expense of taking a bed for them for two weeks and that he would cut her throat rather than her have anybody else'.

Margaret Jones had then asked Jonathan Heywood, 'for 14 shillings to pay for her to leave Manchester and set up in Rochdale'. Heywood agreed to give her the money, 'having convinced the deceased that he had placed the banns for them to be married in Rochdale on 25 July'. On the following Monday, Heywood avoided Jones' sons and sneaked into her room for the last time, leaving at about 5am.

Then, according to Charlotte Albinson, before departing for Rochdale, 'Heywood stole a razor from an elderly man in Manchester.'

*Blackwater Street narrowed at the top towards Half-Moon Yard.*
Rochdale Local Studies Library collection

Finally a chemist testified that spots on Jonathan Heywood's shirt were blood.

The outcome of the inquest was a foregone conclusion: 'Wilful Murder' and a trial date was set. William, or more accurately Christopher, Martin was released into a less hostile environment, presumably keeping a wary eye out for his estranged brother, James.

The prisoner was taken to the railway station on the following day bound for Liverpool Assizes. Not, however, without incident. Thousands packed the streets, 'groaning and booing' and the prison wagon containing Heywood, with Superintendent Jervis at the reins, was forced off the road and into a lamp-post. Jervis 'set the horse galloping down Toad Lane, flying across the town bridge to arrive with a thunder of hooves at the railway station'.

The crowd at the station, 'howled in fury' as Jonathan Heywood, boarding the train, was seen to laugh and joke with his captors and wave to someone in the crowd.

The trial took place at Liverpool on 7 December 1855. Hundreds had travelled from Rochdale on special excursion trains and the court was 'crowded to excess'. Christopher Martin was in attendance and there was general agreement that 'he resembled the accused, both facially and in stature'.

Heywood's suntan had faded and 'he stood pale and dejected but still manifesting a stolid indifference'. He wore a dirty moleskin waistcoat, a red cotton handkerchief and black cord trousers. The Crown Prosecutor pointed to Heywood and addressed the jury: 'All you have to decide is whether the person who went in that room with Margaret Jones deprived her of her life and whether that person is the prisoner at the bar.'

As witness followed witness, it became obvious that Heywood had no defence. The former girlfriend he claimed to have been with on the night of the murder was not produced and his defence counsel could only maintain that the evidence against Heywood was circumstantial. Heywood himself seemed more concerned to prove that he had borrowed, not stolen, the murder weapon, than to establishing his innocence on the capital charge.

The judge summed up and sent the jury to deliberate; which they did . . . for all of seven minutes. Needless to say, Heywood was found guilty. The judge, 'having put on his black cap proceeded to pass the sentence of death upon the prisoner'. Heywood, still proclaiming his innocence, was led from the dock to the condemned cell.

While awaiting execution, Heywood was encouraged to confess by a succession of clergymen. He refused to do so, implying that Christopher Martin may, after all, have been the guilty party. Heywood claimed to have no motive for the murder, a point which had initially bothered the police in Rochdale. He 'wept bitterly when visited by his brother and fourteen-year-old son on the day before the execution'.

On Saturday 5 January, in drizzling rain, Jonathan Heywood was hung at twelve noon in front of nearly 10,000 spectators. At his request, his body lies next to that of Margaret Jones in Rochdale Cemetery.

# Chapter 5

# Bedlam at the Boar's Head

Elements of our next *Foul Deed* bear a resemblance to Stephen King's, *The Shining*. Although the events to be described took place on 7 May 1856, the story begins some thirty years earlier with Rochdale magistrate Samuel Holland.

The Hollands were a wealthy extended family who had lived in the area for centuries. Originally engaged in the flannel trade, succeeding generations had diversified into other areas, until, by the early nineteenth century, they could be found in virtually every sector of industry. Samuel Holland did not come from one of the wealthier branches of the family; having to make his own way in the world, he set up as a tallow chandler, a manufacturer of candles.

His business was located originally on New Wall above the river and the stinking dregs from the animal fats he used were dumped directly into the waters below.

A visitor to the town in 1836 described the River Roch as 'a thick curdled mass, putrid with dye and the rotting remains of animal carcasses'. But, as the phrase goes: 'Where there's muck there's brass' and Samuel Holland prospered. He rose through the ranks of local society, marrying in 1820 and becoming one of the town's magistrates two years later. He was one of the petitioners who, in 1825, succeeded in persuading the government to grant Rochdale borough status and he continued to be a formidable presence on the bench throughout the 1830s. He socialized with the local gentry and was a close friend to Clement Royds, High Sherriff of Lancashire.

In the early 1830s, however, Samuel Holland had an affair with a Sarah Taylor from Coldwall Brow, Spotland who bore him an illegitimate son. Given the closeted nature of the town, this was not something that could be kept secret, but neither was it a matter for discussion in polite society. Samuel Holland's family life continued as before, untroubled by the responsibili-

*Samuel Holland's candle factory, Wheelpit Court – 'Where there's muck there's brass.'*
Rochdale Local Studies Library collection

ties of parenthood.

The boy, James, was not, as often happened, sent away for an education, but lived in some level of comfort with his mother. Sarah Taylor worked as a servant earning a modest wage, and it was widely believed that Samuel Holland contributed to the expense of raising the boy. Certainly, upon his death in 1848, he left James a considerable amount of money, described by the press as 'a small fortune'.

James Taylor, who had been a casual labourer and later a weaver, probably need never have worked again. He had always been a heavy drinker, boasting that 'he was the only man standing after a night of ale', so it may have been tempting but it was probably not the wisest career move, when, using part of his inheritance, Taylor bought the *Boar's Head Inn* on Baillie Street.

His drinking did not stop then, or after his marriage in 1850, or indeed following the birth of the couple's five children. By the time of the birth of a new baby on 17 April 1856, Taylor was drinking all day and every day. He was also displaying symptoms of advanced alcoholism, including paranoia and delirium tremens. His wife, Martha, 'went in fear of her life' and regularly sought refuge at her sister's beer-house on Toad Lane.

On the morning of 7 May 1856 Taylor was, even by his own standards, in a bad way. By 10am he was roaring drunk, screaming at Martha that 'she would not see the day out'. His wife ran upstairs, grabbed her shawl, into which she bundled her seven-week-old baby and raced down the stairs and out of the back door. She 'ran without stopping to her sister's on Toad Lane as if her life depended upon it'. As indeed it did.

The beer-house was run by William Barnish and his wife Elizabeth, Martha Taylor's sister. The couple were used to Martha running to them for protection, but this time seemed different. According to Martha, James Taylor was 'mad with rage and violence would surely follow, both for herself and the children'.

Martha calmed down sufficiently during the afternoon to help out in the beer-house then at around eight o' clock she was 'seized with dread' as a familiar figure appeared in the doorway.

James Taylor, however, appeared sober, 'politely asking Martha to return to the *Boar's Head* and help out with the chores'.

Martha was sceptical. She had been in this situation before; meekly returning home only to be screamed at, punched and kicked as her husband became increasingly drunk.

James Taylor appealed to William Barnish, saying that he could hardly run the *Boar's Head* on his own. To Martha's dismay, Barnish agreed but, realizing that his sister-in-law had been more than usually frightened, suggested that two of his regulars, Thomas Healey and John Brierley, should accompany the Taylors back to the *Boar's Head.*

The pair, who had only recently arrived and had not yet had the opportunity to buy a drink, agreed, saying that 'an ale was an ale wherever it was drunk'. This observation was not to prove entirely accurate. James Taylor said nothing on the way back up Baillie Street. When the party arrived at the *Boar's Head,* he

*Courtyard adjacent to the* Boar's Head Tavern.
Rochdale Local Studies Library collection

went upstairs in search of his four older children. Failing to find them, he accused his wife of 'spiriting them away'. Martha Taylor denied this and Thomas Healey stepped between them, telling Taylor to keep his voice down as there were customers at the bar. Taylor pushed past him to the serving area.

It was at about ten o'clock that Thomas Blomley, whose wife worked for the Barnishes and who had also been asked by Elizabeth Barnish to keep an eye on her sister, entered the pub. Thomas Healey and John Brierley had not yet had a drink, so James Taylor served all three with a pint of ale.

The trio sat down and each took a long pull at his beer. Having downed half of their drinks, Healey and Brierley stopped simultaneously, shouting to Taylor that the beer was bad. Blomley, who had finished most of his in a single draft, threw his head back coughing and spluttering. Healey began vomiting and fell heavily on to the stone floor, 'where he writhed in agony'.

Thomas Blomley dashed around the table and tried to help Healey to his feet. Somehow he got him standing and, doubled up in pain, 'still heaving mucus and bile', Healey was led outside by one of the customers. Now John Brierley staggered forward, grabbing the table for support and sending tankards and glasses crashing to the floor. He was too dizzy to stand unaided and he too had to be helped out of the pub. Blomley too began to be affected. 'He could no longer see, but making his way unsteadily out of the inn', struggled back to the Barnish's beer-house on Toad Lane.

Reeling like a drunkard, it took him nearly twenty minutes to reach his destination. Having startled everyone by tumbling down the steps of the beer-house and slumping to the ground in a heap, Blomley began to 'suffer from awful diarrhoea and a need to go out for the potty'. He was carried into the courtyard where he was 'attended to' by Elizabeth Barnish.

Thomas Blomley was incoherent, unable to tell anyone what had happened to him. His wife Anne knew only that he had been to the *Boar's Head*. She set off to investigate.

Anne Blomley arrived to find the hotel in turmoil. James Taylor was no longer in evidence but there was an upturned table and broken glass on the floor and a recent arrival told her that he thought some men had earlier been poisoned.

Like Martha Taylor before her that day, Anne Blomley ran non-stop back to Toad Lane. Drinking in the beer-house was political agent Peter Johnson who, upon being told of the suspected poisonings, went to the Infirmary to seek medical assistance. He returned with a Mr Pitman, a visiting surgeon from Manchester, who 'set about to try and rescue poor Thomas Blomley and steady his convulsions'. Two other surgeons were despatched to find the other victims of Taylor's poison.

Meanwhile, back at the *Boar's Head*, James Taylor had gone berserk. At around ten o'clock, immediately prior to Anne Blomley's visit, he had kicked open the door of a storeroom at the back of the pub, emerging with a heavy axe. He put the handle of the axe under his coat, ran up the stairs to the first floor, paused to catch his breath and tore up a second staircase to a bedroom at the end of a tiny landing.

The room was rented by William Kershaw who had lodged at the inn for some six months. Taylor shouted for Kershaw to open the door but got no response. He rapped at the door with the handle of the axe. Still no reply. Taylor hammered the door again, and then hefted the axe-head with all his might, 'splintering the wood and splitting the upper panel in two'. He kicked open the shattered door, and entered axe in hand, but the room was empty.

Taylor dropped his weapon against the wall and descended the staircase to the taproom.

Despite the frantic events of that night, he was about to have a customer. John Chadwick was considered a harmless eccentric. A regular at the pub, he was a fan of the races and had recently been to the meeting at Chester. When he entered the *Boar's Head*, he heard Taylor, 'screaming in a very frightening manner at his wife, who was sat stock-still in a rocking-chair'. Taylor had realized that his four older children, who he had earlier accused his wife of 'spiriting away', were indeed nowhere in the building. He was demanding to know where they were hidden.

John Chadwick attempted to divert Taylor's attention by telling him about his day at Chester races and gradually Taylor calmed down. The two men chatted for ten minutes then, in mid-conversation, Taylor walked to the fireplace, picked up the poker and began to stoke the coals. Suddenly, without warning, 'he twisted the poker, a big heavy weapon, around, firmly grasped it in his hand, hefted it on to his shoulder and dealt his wife the most sickening blow on top of her head, which felled her to the ground, her head being laid open with the most frightful wound'.

Taylor then whirled around and swung the poker at his baby. Chadwick pounced on Taylor's arm deflecting the impact on to his own elbow and received a barrage of blows to the head and body.

There had been enough activity at the *Boar's Head* that night to alert an army but as yet no police were in the vicinity. Help, however, was on its way. Peter Johnson, whose father had once been Chief Constable of Rochdale, had wakened Sergeant Jeffries and told him of the attempted poisonings.

Jeffries got dressed and hurried to the *Boar's Head* to be greeted by a scene of biblical chaos. John Chadwick was yelling at the top of his voice, Martha Taylor was shrieking, the baby was screaming and James Taylor was roaring like a maddened bull. Jeffries took charge, grabbing Taylor around the throat. Not subtle, but effective.

John Chadwick staggered out of the building to find a doctor for Martha Taylor, leaving Jeffries with James Taylor and the baby. Jeffries had no handcuffs with him and had to guard the infant until the arrival of Mr Pitman, the surgeon and Elizabeth Barnish. Finally James Taylor could be taken to the police station and charged.

It was two o'clock on Thursday morning when Taylor and Sergeant Jeffries left the *Boar's Head* and walked wearily up Yorkshire Street towards the police offices, but the drama was not yet over.

Having no handcuffs to restrain the prisoner, Jeffries gripped Taylor by the back of his overcoat collar as they made their slow progress up the street. Taylor was shuffling, although whether from fatigue or reluctance to reach his destination, Jeffries could not tell.

Twice, Taylor reached for something in his coat pocket, then changed his mind and walked on with his hands by his side. Jeffries pulled Taylor towards him, 'to tell him to get a move on' and spotted Taylor putting something in his mouth. Realizing that Taylor was drinking from a small bottle, Jeffries grabbed the prisoners' arm and wrenched the bottle from his lips. It fell to the ground empty.

Stooping to pick it from the road, Jeffries saw that Taylor was smiling and grabbing his collar again practically frogmarched him through the door of the police offices. On the bottle that Taylor had drained was a label bearing the legend 'Whitehead Druggist' and underneath, 'Essential Oil of Almonds'.

The long-suffering Mr Pitman was sent for and he arrived ten minutes later, 'looking tired and concerned'.

He went to the room where the prisoner was being kept to find him in an 'advanced stage of poisoning, vomiting a terrible bile, screaming and crying out in anguish, his interior burning as if by acid'. Try as he may, there was nothing Pitman could do, although it took Taylor over an hour to die an agonizing death.

Later, quoting from his pharmacopeia Pitman confirmed what Sergeant Jeffries had suspected: 'Essential Oil of Almonds is a yellow distillation of almonds of an agreeable odour but as sold, highly poisonous containing 14 per cent of prussic acid. It destroys in the same manner as prussic acid and dependent upon its concentration can kill almost instantly.'

Mr Pitman slumped into a chair. It had been a hectic few hours but at least his other patients, including Martha Taylor, had survived their ordeal: 'Her wound was grave but not lethal, and it was likely she would make a full recovery.'

The inquest on James Taylor took place on the evening of Saturday 10 May at the *Tweedale Hotel*, Baillie Street. The witnesses included Thomas Healey and John Brierley but Thomas Blomley, 'although not in danger of his life, was too weak to testify'. Martha Taylor was 'granted permission not to attend the proceedings'.

Thomas Healey and John Brieley gave their evidence but it was the third witness, John Chadwick who was able to shed most light on a case the prosecution described as: 'pregnant with the wildest horror'. He introduced himself as 'John Chadwick, age forty-three, a resident of Shawclough' and stated that he was a regular at the *Boar's Head* and 'knew the domestic situation there tolerably well'. He may have been widely regarded as an eccentric but it was Chadwick who had advised William Kershaw, the lodger at the *Boar's Head*, to make himself scarce on the night of 7 May.

Martha Taylor had spoken to Chadwick at length on the evening of 6 May and had told him that she was frightened for her own life and for those of her five children. James Taylor had threatened her before, she said, but now 'he seemed intent on carrying through his evil'. Martha Taylor also revealed to Chadwick that 'she had made arrangements for the safety of her children'.

As she later told the police: on the morning of 7 May, so fuddled was James Taylor that he was unaware of Martha Taylor's youngest sister, Hannah, creeping into the pub and leading the four older children through the rear door, across the courtyard to safety. The baby, however, was with her mother at the beer shop in Toad Lane.

Chemist John Whitehead, who also gave evidence at the inquest, confirmed that Taylor had bought the 'Essential Oil of Almonds' at his shop and that he had warned Taylor of 'its injurious effects if taken by mouth rather than used as scent'. Taylor's actions were clearly premeditated and it was fortunate for Brierley, Healey and Blomley that the dosage Taylor had administered to them had been sufficiently diluted by the beer to do them no permanent damage.

Both Martha Taylor and John Chadwick were convinced that something terrible was going to happen on 7 May, but even they could not have predicted the ferocity and madness of what was to follow. James Taylor had been prepared to kill John Brierley, Thomas Healey, Thomas Blomley, William Kershaw and John Chadwick in order to implement his murderous plan for his wife and five children.

*Toad Lane, near the Barnish's beer-shop, where Martha Taylor fled from her husband.* Rochdale Local Studies Library collection

# CHAPTER 6

# The Rochdale Garrotting Panic

A garrotte was a piece of string or wire 'wrapped around the throat and pulled or twisted to effect a strangulation of the victim'. Originally garrotting formed part of the state punishment apparatus in Spain, but the method was soon adopted by robbers and murderers throughout Europe.

In 1851 London experienced a series of violent street robberies carried out by small bands of travelling thieves. Occasionally wire was used to semi-strangle the victim, but more usually the perpetrator would find an isolated passer-by, wrap a stiff arm around his throat and choke him. An accomplice would rifle the victim's pockets, stealing money, watches or other valuables. Gradually the term, 'garrotting' began to be applied to any attack from behind, or any robbery where extreme physical violence was employed.

These attacks, which triggered massive public concern in the metropolis, spread rapidly to the rest of the country. Manchester experienced an outbreak of garrotting in 1851 and soon similar assaults were being carried out in Rochdale and the other cotton towns.

The phenomenon created an atmosphere of near hysteria. The attacks were swift and brutal and the perpetrators faded into the night, leaving the police as powerless as the victims.

In February 1856, a travelling salesman, John Hibbert, had taken lodgings in a beer house on Packer Street. He had never visited Rochdale before. Had he done so, he would have realized that the area around Packer Street was not a safe place to wander at night and he certainly would not have been in the *Badger Inn* at 10pm on Saturday 19 February.

Packer Street led via the Parish Church Steps to Church Lane and the area known as the Gank, 'an area of depravity, crime and pestilence where nasty ladies ply their trade'. Even in the 1850s police patrols stopped at the *Flying Horse Hotel* at the foot of the hill.

*Looking up Packer Street towards the notorious 'Gank'.*
Rochdale Local Studies Library collection

The area consisted of a collection of low-roofed hovels pressed so closely together that it was possible to run, leaping from roof to roof, should the necessity arise. Slops, household rubbish and human excrement were thrown into the street and dogs scavenged unmolested in the filth. It was, according to one magistrate, 'a sink of iniquity, more vile than anywhere else in the realm'.

As John Hibbert left the *Badger Inn* at 10.30pm to return to his lodgings, he noticed that he was being followed by two women, 'dressed for the night'. He made his way unsteadily down Packer Street, intending to enter his lodgings, but 'found his passage blocked by the two women who seemed very determined to stop him from gaining admission'. One of the women said something 'very offensive' and Hibbert turned and ran as best he could into the safety of the (comparatively) respectable *Flying Horse*.

To his consternation, the women followed him and stood by the bar, 'whispering to each other and casting frequent glances in his direction'. Eventually his pursuers appeared to tire of their vigil and left, one 'daring to wave as if she knew the man well'.

Hibbert rose and walked through the bar to the side entrance and out into the courtyard . . . where the women were waiting for him. One was hidden behind the door and 'putting a piece of piping around his neck, pulled mightily, strangling him'. The other removed his purse and watch. Hibbert fell to the ground and his attackers fled through the courtyard and back up Packer Street.

Hibbert staggered to his feet and raised the alarm. The police were called, enquiries were made and two women, Sally Clegg and Margaret Chadwick were arrested. Hibbert was presented with a line-up from which to identify his assailants. He made the wrong choice selecting, 'two women of outstanding character' and left the town disillusioned, 'vowing never to return'.

If John Hibbert was naively unaware of the dangers lurking in Church Lane, James Turner should have known better. Turner, from Bacup, was a prosecutor in the debtors' court who visited Rochdale on a regular basis.

On Thursday 10 March 1856, he had been pursuing a debt in the County Court at Rochdale when he 'got into a house of ill-fame in Church Lane'. Firstly he had his pockets picked to the tune of £3, 8 shillings and 6 pence, then someone stole the currant-bread his wife had wrapped for him in a linen handker-chief, then, 'after he had been tumbled out of the house between twelve o' clock and one o' clock on Friday morning, he was strangled from behind and robbed of his pocket-watch'.

The pocket-watch was never recovered but Maria Johnson and Dennis Howarth were eventually found guilty of the thefts carried out within the brothel. The defence's assertion that the £3, 8 shillings and 6 pence had been given by Turner to Maria Johnson as payment for services rendered raised a few eyebrows in court. The average weekly wage in those days was about £1.

Johnson and Howarth were each sentenced to three months hard labour and James Turner returned to Bacup a sadder and (perhaps) wiser man.

At least the two previous victims survived their visit to Rochdale. The next target of the 'Rochdale Garrotters' was not so fortunate. Samuel Bell, a 48-year-old coach trimmer from Gateshead, was working in Rochdale on a short-term contract with Renshaw's Coachbuilders on Acker Street. He got on well with his fellow workers and, through his trade union affiliations, had become friendly with Simon Chapman, secretary of the Coachmakers' Society.

On 26 April 1856 Chapman asked Bell to join himself and his wife for a Saturday night drink at the *Coach and Horses Hotel* on Lord Street. Chapman's wife was to meet them later, so the two men decided to drink spirits, 'as a sign of friendship', before she arrived.

They had each bought a round of whisky and Bell was about to go to the bar when they became aware of a man standing close to the table, clearly eavesdropping on their conversation. Samuel Bell inquired sarcastically if the stranger would care to join them and 'was astonished when he proceeded to do so'. The stranger also took Bell up on his equally sarcastic offer of a drink, 'watching Bell carefully as he paid at the bar'.

After two awkward rounds, the second one bought by Simon Chapman, their new companion, who had never bothered introducing himself, suddenly stood up and left. Chapman's wife arrived and the two men, who in retrospect found the incident highly entertaining, told her 'the tale of the thirsty stranger, to general laughter'. At twelve o'clock everyone agreed that they had had enough to drink and they left the *Coach and Horses* to go their separate ways.

*Lord Street, towards the* Coach and Horses, *where Samuel Bell encountered the* '*thirsty stranger*'. Rochdale Local Studies Library collection

As Samuel Bell was walking along Baillie Street towards his lodgings he was suddenly kicked from behind. His right ankle above his boot took most of the impact and his leg gave way sending him sprawling to the ground. He struggled to get to his feet but one or two men, in the dark he couldn't be certain, began to kick him with clogs. He fell back to the floor, unable to protect himself. He couldn't cry for help because one assailant was aiming blows at his face and the more he tried to twist and turn, the more violent the attack became.

Someone rifled through the pockets of his waistcoat and took a tobacco box inscribed with his name and occupation, a needle case, a pair of steel-framed blue-lensed glasses and a small amount of money. The thief, or thieves, then went for Bell's purse, which was in the other pocket of his waistcoat and contained around 12 shillings.

When Bell raised his hands in resistance, someone pulled out a knife and slashed both hands so badly that 'they were mangled in such a way that he would not carry out his employment again'. At that point, a passer-by witnessed the attack and the assailants disappeared. In fact the witness could only swear to seeing one man but the footsteps clattering on the setts, 'were loud enough for two'.

Samuel Bell was supported, his savaged hands pouring with blood, to the Infirmary where he, along with Simon Chapman, was interviewed by the police. Neither man could furnish a description of the stranger in the *Coach and Horses*, except that he was 'perhaps about 5 feet 7 inches tall, not very stout with his hair if anything, of a sandy colour'.

Samuel Bell returned to Gateshead on 10 May 1856, telling his mother that 'thanks to Rochdale he was a murdered man'. He said that he was so drunk on the night of the attack that he couldn't describe his attackers, or even guess their number but now he just wanted to stay at home for a few days and recover his strength.

On Friday 16 May, Bell couldn't drag himself out of bed and, despite a doctor being called to his bedside, by the following afternoon he was dead. Although the subsequent inquest could cast no light on the identity of the attackers, it did reveal how brutal the assault had been. According to Dr Barkas of Gateshead, 'there were terrible wounds on the head, the palms of the hand were ruined and clenched and the left thumb was amputated at the first joint. The cause of death,' he concluded, 'was an abscess between the duramater and the skull, the result of a violent fracture.'

The verdict of the inquest was that Samuel Bell had been, 'wilfully murdered by some person or persons whose names are unknown'.

An episode that took place two years after the death of Samuel Bell represented a novel variation on the modus-operandi of the garrotter; an attack on the night train.

The *Manchester–Leeds Railway* had been an outstanding success. Opened in 1842, it provided cheap transport that was not only faster than the road or canal, but was generally considered safer. Until the early 1840s the highways into Manchester were still the haunt of 'footpads, vagabonds and thieves' and highway robbery was a regular hazard.

The early railway rolling stock had been upgraded so that, by the 1850s, single or double compartment coaches offered more comfort than a horse-drawn carriage, but crucially less privacy.

Edward Wainwright was a teacher in the Endowed School at Littleborough. He was also secretary of the Littleborough Mutual Improvement Society. On Thursday, 14 February 1858, Wainwright decided to bank the proceeds of the society: £9, 10 shillings in gold. He caught the train to Rochdale and was walking down Drake Street when he met a man called James Goodwin who owed him a considerable amount of money. The two arranged to meet in Manchester that evening where, Goodwin promised, he would repay the debt.

Wainwright travelled to Manchester and met Goodwin by All Saints Church. Goodwin gave him 30 shillings in silver, which Wainwright put in his purse. He now had £9, 10 shillings in gold and 30 shillings of silver on his person, so he decided against visiting a pub and instead entered a chemist's shop. Here he purchased a bottle of chloroform for his teeth, which, 'were aching badly'.

Walking past Manchester Cathedral on his way back to Victoria Station, Wainwright saw a man 'who appeared extremely drunk' lying on the flagstones. As he passed, the man stood up and reeled against Wainwright, tapping his coat pockets lightly as he did so. Wainwright, fearing the worst, ran across the road, hurriedly entered the station concourse and bought a single ticket to Littleborough.

As he walked to the platform he remembered that he had already purchased a return ticket at Littleborough and turned back to the counter to get a refund. There, behind him was the man from the Cathedral Steps, 'now standing erect and sober'.

Wainwright collected his refund and carefully chose a full double compartment for his journey on the 7.45pm to Leeds, via Rochdale, Littleborough and Todmorden.

Originally there were six passengers in the compartment, two of whom got off at Miles Platting. This was in the days before corridor coaches, so had Wainwright stayed where he was, he probably would have reached his destination safely. However, there was, at the time, a five-minute 'comfort break' at Rochdale so Wainwright 'left the compartment to find the urinal'. As he was stepping down from the train he saw 'leaning out of a carriage window two or three compartments off, the man from the Cathedral Steps'.

To his dismay, as he entered the toilet block Wainwright saw the man get out of his compartment, walk along the platform and board the train again; climbing into the compartment Wainwright had just vacated.

Edward Wainwright waited until the train was about to depart and then walked down the platform and got into an

*The Manchester–Leeds Railway, close to the Summit Tunnel at Littleborough.*
Rochdale Local Studies Library collection

empty single compartment. Seconds later he was horrified to see the door open and the man from Manchester easing himself into the compartment. The stranger sat down directly opposite him. Before Wainwright could disembark, the train pulled out of the station and gathered speed.

As the train sped through Smithybridge, Wainwright's worst fears were realized. The man leaned forward and grabbed Wainwright violently by the throat with his left hand. His right hand went to his coat pocket. The assailant drew out a pistol and put it to Edward Wainwright's head saying, 'If you speak a word or stir, I'll blow your bloody brains to hell.' Wainwright promptly fainted.

When he came round he was lying on the carriage floor with his attacker kneeling next to him. The man still had the gun pointed at Wainwright's head but now in his left hand he held the bottle of chloroform that Wainwright had bought in Manchester. Pulling the cork with his teeth, the assailant forced the bottle into Wainwright's mouth and poured chloroform down his throat. Wainwright pushed the bottle away but fell unconscious again just as the train roared out of the Summit Tunnel.

When the train stopped at Walsden, Edward Wainwright was found insensible on the floor of the carriage, but there was no sign of his attacker, or of the purse containing £11 that had been in Wainwright's pocket. Also missing was Wainwright's gold watch.

Edward Wainwright was taken to Todmorden police station where he learned that he was only one of several passengers to have been assaulted and robbed on the railway that week.

Around Wainwright's neck was a livid red mark caused by his attacker's hand gripping his throat, together with two distinct indentations left by a pair of rings. To the police, Wainwright confidently described his attacker 'as having been about 5 feet 10 inches tall with a very peculiar cast to his left eye'.

The description was circulated by telegram and the following day Joshua Smith, a Liverpool detective assigned to the Mersey boats, spotted Michael Brannon, 'a known felon,' leaving the boat-train. Brannon had recently had treatment for an infection on his left eye and was sporting 'a large and fancy eye patch'. He also wore two heavy rings on the fingers of his left hand.

Smith arrested Brannon 'on suspicion of murderous assault' and Edward Wainwright was brought to Bridewell in Liverpool to identify his attacker in a line-up. This he initially failed to do because, although the prisoner's clothes and hat matched those of his attacker and Brannon's infected eye, 'seemed familiar to him', Wainwright had described his attacker as being about 5 feet 10 inches tall. Brannon was a mere 5 foot 3.

Wainwright consulted with Superintendent Storey from Rochdale who had accompanied him to Liverpool, then went back to the line-up and touched Brannon on the shoulder.

Much to Brannon's disgust, he was transferred all the way to Rochdale to appear in front of the magistrates and then back to Liverpool for the trial at the Assizes.

The trial of 'Michael Brannon, 40, hairdresser from Liverpool' began at Liverpool Assizes on Monday 29 March. The prosecution related the details of the attack on Wainwright and its aftermath. It was submitted that 'having carried out his murderous assault' Brannon had leapt from the moving train as it slowed before stopping at Walsden.

Thomas Wheeler for the defence was dismissive of the prosecution's case. He said that the discrepancy in height between the attacker as described by Wainwright in his statement and 'the man of very small stature in front of us now' was irreconcilable.

He then attempted to construct an alibi for Brannon by producing 'a series of witnesses of good character'.

The first was a Mathilda Turner who stated that the accused had stayed at her lodging house on the night of the assault and that Michael Brannon had come in at about nine o' clock in the evening and not gone out again. Cross-examined, Turner admitted that in her original statement she had said that Brannon had gone out 'but only for an hour'.

Christopher Hewitt and Peter McDonald both testified on Brannon 's behalf that they were gambling with him in a beer house in Shudehill Manchester until 7pm on 14 February and that Brannon had gone to Victoria Station with them, but had then boarded the train for Liverpool.

The next testimony was interrupted by Michael Brannon who was incensed that his defence counsel had not brought forward someone he considered a vital witness. It transpired that Brannon 's barrister had not been briefed by his attorney and with a few well-chosen words to the defence team, the judge allowed the witness to be called.

Joseph Ormerod, a mechanic from Manchester, testified that Edward Wainwright 'could not have been robbed, because he had pawned his gold watch in Manchester on the afternoon before the alleged attack took place'.

Edward Wainwright was recalled to the stand and denied the allegation. He then related a series of events that he said took place after the robbery. Two weeks before the Liverpool trial a man had met him at Victoria Station Manchester and asked him if his name was Wainwright. When he confirmed that 'indeed it was' the man asked him if he would like his watch back. Wainwright replied that he would like it back very much and was told that if he went to the *Boar's Head Tavern* in Todd Street, Manchester, 'a stranger would ask him the same question and his property would be returned'.

He went straight to the *Boar's Head* and there, waiting for him, was Michael Brannon's star witness, Joseph Ormerod. Ormerod said that Wainwright could have his watch back if he handed over £2 on the spot. Ormerod would then go and fetch the watch from a friend. Wainwright walked out. Even he was not that naïve.

The jury had no doubt about the guilt of Michael Brannon and the judge was determined to make an example, both of him and of his friends in the court. He requested the police to investigate for evidence of 'perjured testimony' in the trial and urged them to bring charges against Joseph Ormerod in particular. Then, turning to Brannon he said: 'We are in a new age of transport and if your crime was passed over lightly no one would be safe. This is a new species of robbery and it is proper that a stop should be put to it at once by a heavy punishment.'

It seemed probable that the judge was going to pass the death sentence and 'Brannon fell against the side of the box in terror' but because of the likelihood that a sentence of death would be commuted upon appeal, the judge opted for 'the heaviest practical punishment that the law provides – transportation for life'.

Michael Brannon was bound for Botany Bay and Edward Wainwright returned, 'with great relief' to the security of his teaching post in Littleborough.

The frequency of incidents of garrotting did not diminish, either in Rochdale or elsewhere. Such was the level of public concern that in 1863 the government introduced the *Security from Violence Act*, more commonly known as the 'Garrotters' Act', which, 'for those offences meriting less than transportation', punished those committing violent street robberies with 'a lengthy prison sentence and fifty strokes of birching'.

# CHAPTER 7

# 'Dirty Old Town'

*I found my love 'neath the gasworks wall*
*Dreamed a dream by the old canal*
*Kissed my girl by the factory wall*
*Dirty old town, dirty old town*

EWAN MACCOLL

Flanked by high cotton mills, the Rochdale canal passes under Oldham Road at Lock Bridge. Here it originally branched into two sections, the main channel flowing towards Belfield, Smithybridge and Littleborough with the spur cutting through to the wharves at the Richard Street Basin. At Lock Bridge the waters where the branches met were turbulent and the towpath, under the shadow of Oldham Road, was dank and gloomy. It was the place for chance encounters and secret assignations.

On Tuesday 9 April 1861, Edmund Travis was walking the towpath towards Lock Bridge. He watched three barges queuing to access the town lock, their hauling lines hanging loosely in the water. When the line for the third barge was tightened, Travis saw it snag a heavy object and bring it slowly to the surface. In the half-light, Travis could see a dark shape floating by the prow of the barge and yelled to the boatman to join him. Together they ran up the canal bank and saw the body of a young woman, hair streaming around her, bobbing on the water's edge.

The two dragged the body on to the towpath and called the police. The first officer on the scene, PC Dunlop, searched the woman's clothing for any form of identification. In the pocket of her dress he found £2, 14 shillings and 3 pence and a sodden scrap of paper bearing the address: 'Moston Buildings Harpurhey'.

Superintendent Pickering had arrived in the police van and arranged for the removal of the body. After three hours of tedious door-to-door enquiries, he finally knocked on the door

*'I kissed my girl by the factory wall . . .' The view towards Lock Bridge, Oldham Road.*
Rochdale Local Studies Library collection

of a Martha Turner, who told him with some reluctance that she thought 'Ellen Garside of 14 Milkstone Road might have gone missing again.'

Pickering made his way to Milkstone Road, rapped on the door of Number 14 and waited. The door opened to reveal a mild looking man in his mid-thirties with a young girl of around ten at his side. The man greeted Pickering with the words: 'It's my wife isn't it?'

The man, Joseph Garside, told Pickering that he was a bookkeeper with the Merchants' Company. He had married Ellen Horsfall on 8 May 1850. The couple had two children, Eliza Ann and Samuel. Following the birth of the boy, Joseph went to seek his fortune in America, arranging to send for his family when he had found a job and a place to live. He returned to Rochdale after a year, disillusioned with the New World and took up his former employment with the Merchants' Company. The family moved to a house in Great George Street where they took in three lodgers.

Then, on 12 September 1860, said Joseph Garside, his wife Ellen disappeared for five months, 'and took this 'un with her'. The girl nodded. 'She came back to me this February,' Joseph Garside continued, 'and we were as right as rain and moved in with my mother. She disappeared again on Easter Monday, the first of April and I went looking for her.'

That was eight days previously. Superintendent Pickering, half-convinced that Joseph Garside was 'a bit simple or worse' questioned the girl, Eliza Ann, at length. What he discovered was complex and confusing but at least he had gleaned sufficient to present to the Coroner at the following day's inquest.

The inquest took place on Wednesday 10 April at the *Brown Cow Inn*, Milkstone Road. Joseph and Eliza Ann Garside, having positively identified the deceased as 'Ellen Garside age thirty-two' both gave evidence. Again, it was nine-year-old Eliza Ann who caught the attention of Superintendent Pickering when, for the first time, she mentioned staying with her mother and a man called Mr Roberts at the house of a Mrs Parkinson in Harpurhey, Manchester.

A verdict of drowning, but not suicide was reached by the inquest jury. Pickering hurriedly left the pub. He was eager to locate Mrs Parkinson in Harpurhey, confident that she would be found at the address written on the note in the drowned woman's pocket. He took with him an intriguing letter recently sent to Ellen Garside in Rochdale, and boarded the train for Manchester.

Seven months earlier, on 12 September 1860, Ellen Garside had made the same journey with her daughter. It was a bright early autumn morning and Ellen was simultaneously terrified and elated. A combination of circumstances had precipitated her flight from Rochdale. She was having an affair, not she had to admit, for the first time and she was receiving anonymous letters threatening to expose her infidelity to her husband. On the positive side, she was travelling to Manchester to meet her lover.

Whilst Joseph Garside had been living in America, Ellen had shared a room with one of her lodgers, Edmond Howarth. Upon Joseph's return, Edmond Howarth had suddenly left Rochdale and Joseph had picked up on the inevitable rumours and innuendo. He questioned Ellen but 'appeared totally indifferent to the affair and let the matter drop'.

Ellen was not convinced that her husband would be so placid and understanding a second time.

The anonymous letters were, as far as Ellen could judge, written in a female hand, which made sense as she had recently fallen out with her neighbour, Mary Little. Ellen had diverted money intended for Mary Little into her own purse and the anonymous letters had begun shortly afterwards.

The first communication described how Ellen had been seen in Poulton 'on the arm of a tall handsome man', the second how the two were observed 'in passionate circumstances at a race meeting'.

Ellen suspected that similar letters had been sent to her husband. She had arranged to pay off Mary Little using another neighbour, Frances Karberry, as a go-between, but was not confident that the anonymous letters would cease.

Ellen Garside had prepared for her flight to Manchester. On the previous Friday she had had arranged lodgings for 'Mr and Mrs Roberts and their daughter Eliza Ann' with a Mrs Whitcombe of 20 Colleyhurst Street.

From that address, on 12 September Ellen wrote a note, bearing no postmark, to her husband in Rochdale. In the letter, Ellen warned Joseph that he would shortly receive anonymous correspondence accusing her of infidelity. She had left Rochdale, she said, because 'she could not bear the shame of such gossip and would soon be travelling abroad with a Mr and Mrs Roberts'.

Having made a nominal effort to trace his wife, Joseph left Great George Street with his son and moved in with his mother and her two lodgers at 14 Milkstone Road.

Meanwhile in Manchester, Ellen Garside, now known as Ellen Roberts was living with her daughter in Colleyhurst Street, where she was joined by the mysterious Mr Roberts on Wednesday and Saturday nights. On 13 September 'the whole Roberts family went out in search of a pub and came to Moston Buildings, the house of a Mrs Parkinson, who invited them in for drinks, which they paid for and for which they expressed their gratitude'.

This idyllic existence continued for seven weeks, with 'Mr

Roberts visiting regularly and sharing a room with his "wife", whilst their daughter slept with the children of the house'.

Then, on 23 October Ellen Garside received a letter from 'Mr Roberts', saying that he had been forced to leave his job. That Saturday, he failed to arrive at Colleyhurst Street. In a flood of tears, Ellen told Mrs Whitcombe that she had been abandoned; that her husband had gone to America without her. On the following day, 'Ellen Roberts and her daughter left 20 Colleyhurst Street'.

The pair went directly to Mrs Parkinson at Moston Buildings, Harpurhey, where they had enjoyed drinks as a family the previous month. To Ellen Garside's immense relief, 'Mr Roberts' had not abandoned her, tracking the Garsides down in Harpurhey the following Wednesday. Here, the living arrangements continued as before, but a new intensity was added to the relationship by the couple's constant talk of emigration to America. The Parkinsons became close to their new lodgers, sharing drinks and food and joining in their fantasies of a new life in the USA.

Then, towards the end of January 1861, Ellen became depressed, saying to Mrs Parkinson on more than one occasion: 'I know it will happen, I shall bring it on'. On 2 February she had a miscarriage. She had been three months pregnant.

Joseph Garside still had not visited Manchester to search for his wife, but he had made some enquiries as to her whereabouts amongst friends and neighbours. He had learned from a James Schofield that Ellen was rumoured to have been seen with a man on Shudehill Market. Garside went to long-standing family friend, John Warburton to ask if he had heard the same story. Warburton had spent some time in America after Joseph Garside had returned to England and the pair had become close, regularly swapping tales of the New World over drinks with Ellen and Eliza Ann. Warburton said he was aware of no rumours to the effect that Ellen was in Manchester, nor, he said, 'could he believe the way she had treated her husband after all these years'.

So Joseph Garside was none the wiser, until 4 February 1861 when, out of the blue, he received a letter from his wife saying that she was coming home the following day. This she did, looking 'ill and tired'.

Ellen and Eliza Ann were reunited with Joseph, his mother and young Samuel at 14 Milkstone Road and family life resumed as if the events of the last five months had never happened.

Joseph Garside's Buddha-like serenity was undented; he 'readily accepted his wife's story that she had lodged innocently with the Parkinsons in Manchester to escape the shame generated by the poison-pen letters'.

Then, after a month of blissful reconciliation including reunions with John Warburton and other friends, more anonymous correspondence arrived for Ellen, which, this time, Joseph Garside intercepted. Following Ellen Garside's drowning, Joseph passed the letter to the police and it was this piece of evidence that, after the inquest, Superintendent Pickering took with him to Harpurhey.

Letter in pocket, Pickering had reached Moston Buildings, Harpurhey in the early afternoon, confirming that the address on the note in Ellen Garside's dress was indeed that of her former landlady, Mrs Parkinson. Pickering showed Mrs Parkinson the letter he had brought from the inquest and asked her to return with him to Rochdale, his suspicions concerning the identity of the mysterious Mr Roberts confirmed.

Back in Rochdale, Superintendent Pickering drove Mrs Parkinson to Davenport's Builders' Yard and reined the horses to a halt in front of a group of stonemasons. Prompted by Pickering, Mrs Parkinson approached one of the men and said 'good morning Mr Roberts'. The man turned 'as pale as a sheet'. It was Joseph Garside's friend and confidant John Warburton.

The letter to Ellen Garside was a love letter from Warburton, berating her for having missed an assignation and signed, 'J.W.' Superintendent Pickering had made the connection that had apparently eluded Joseph Garside: 'J.W.' and the mysterious 'Mr Roberts' were one and the same, Ellen Garside's lover, John Warburton.

The police had been busy in Rochdale and had accumulated sufficient evidence to arrest Warburton 'for the Wilful Murder of Ellen Garside'. The case against 'John Warburton, widower, aged thirty-five of Oldham Road, Rochdale' was brought before the magistrates on 18 April 1861.

The first witness called to give evidence at the hearing was Joseph Garside. He described how his wife had left him the previous September, having received a series of anonymous letters and that he had not seen her or his daughter, Eliza Ann, again for five months.

Mrs Parkinson confirmed that Ellen Garside and someone she now knew to be John Warburton had lived together as man and wife at her house in Harpurhey and that the couple had even 'visited' the Parkinsons for a night as recently as March

1861, a month after Ellen Garside had returned home to her husband in Rochdale.

Eliza Ann testified that her mother had encouraged her to call John Warburton, 'father' while they lived in Manchester and then related how Ellen Garside had walked out of the house 'in good spirits' at around 7.30pm on Monday 1 April to go to her sister's house, but had never returned. Joseph Garside, said Eliza Ann, had not been present when her mother had left but had arrived home shortly afterwards. At about eight o'clock he left the house to look for his wife.

Recalled to the witness-stand, Joseph Garside confirmed that his wife had disappeared for a second time on 1 April and that he had searched for her, even going to the house of John Warburton, who he thought may have had contact with her earlier. On the following day he had gone to Manchester looking for Ellen but had failed to locate her and returned home, hearing nothing until Superintendent Pickering had knocked on his door on 9 April.

The police then introduced a number of witnesses who finally shed some light on the fateful events of 1 April. According to the landlady of the *Bridge Inn*, at 9pm Ellen Garside and John Warburton were drinking brandy in the bar parlour. The couple left the inn and were spotted walking arm-in-arm down the canal towpath in the pouring rain, stopping to shelter on the narrow towpath beneath the bridge.

Sitting in the cabin of her canal barge, Mary Sykes had heard what she took to be a woman's scream above the drumming of the rain. The cry was heard by three other witnesses. Then, apart from the pounding of the rain, there was silence. Suddenly, she heard a loud splash followed by a man's voice crying from the water: 'Help, murder!' Three bargees and gardener, John Horrocks, ran along the towpath. Seeing through the sheeting rain a man struggling in the water, Horrocks extended a pole to him and dragged him to the bank. As they hauled him out, all four shouted: 'Is there a woman with you?' The man did not reply. 'Were you alone? Is there a woman in there?' repeated Horrocks, but the man turned and refusing all assistance, walked into the night. Each witness identified that man as John Warburton.

Surgeon William Sellers, who had made the post-mortem examination, then testified that there were slight bruise-marks on the arms of the deceased, but his conclusion was that Ellen Garside had died 'as a result of a combination of terror and

*'Where the body was found' – Lock Bridge.* Rochdale Local Studies Library collection

drowning'.

The prisoner, Warburton, was cautioned against making a statement by his solicitor, James Hartley, and was committed for trial at the South Lancashire Assizes.

At the subsequent hearing on 14 August 1861, the Crown called two additional witnesses, both of whom swore to having seen John Warburton on the Sunday following his rescue from the canal, two days before Ellen Garside's body was discovered. Each stated that they had seen Warburton walk to the bridge over the canal and, shading his eyes against the glare, stare hard at the water. He dropped to his knees 'appearing to be searching for something beneath the surface of the canal'.

Superintendent Pickering testified that when Warburton was questioned as to his whereabouts on the evening of Monday 1 April, he replied: 'At my house and never out'. Upon being cautioned, he repeated that he had not left home that night. He said the death of Ellen Garside was 'a serious matter which must be looked into but had nothing to do with him'. As for motive,

Superintendent Pickering cited an alleged conversation between Warburton and a James Standish, during which Warburton had complained about the expense and inconvenience of keeping a mistress.

Mr Simon Gray summed up for the Crown by referring to medical evidence that suggested that the lack of water in the deceased's lungs was due to her screaming at the moment of immersal. He submitted that Warburton's reluctance to acknowledge that there was another person in the canal was the result of him having pushed Ellen Warburton from the towpath. 'In fact,' Gray concluded, 'the prisoner had then lost his footing and joined his victim in the water.'

Judge Lord Martin, presiding, was not impressed: 'There are,' he said, 'too many assumptions in this case. Assuming that the prisoner was the man in the public house, assuming that he was in the water, there is nothing beyond assumption to imply that the accused did anything to cause the death of the deceased. We can,' he continued cryptically, 'understand how, given the "assumed" nature of their assignation, the accused would be embarrassed to admit that he was in the vicinity of the canal that night. There is, in short, no evidence to go before the jury. It is not necessary for the defence to present a case.'

The prisoner 'was accordingly acquitted and stood in the dock with a beaming smile on his face'.

Superintendent Pickering may have had his reservations about the outcome of the trial but John Warburton left the court a free man. However, was the death of Ellen Garside just a tragic accident or did Warburton get away with murder? Or did somebody else?

Why did John Warburton shout: 'Help, murder!' as he plunged into the canal? Not presumably to advertise his own crime. Had somebody pushed both him and Ellen Garside into the water?

If so, was that person the long-suffering Joseph Garside who was, by his own admission, out looking for his wife at the time of the incident? Had the worm finally turned?

# CHAPTER 8

# A Slaying at Slattocks

This is the story of two men: one barely out of his teens, the other described as 'old' (he was forty-four). One was murdered, the other was hung. Both were poor and ill-educated. They met at Slattocks outside Rochdale on a warm May morning in 1866.

John Brennan had set out from Waterford in Ireland, not to seek his fortune but to earn enough money to keep his wife Rose and six children from starvation. In his pocket, Brennan carried two references. Each was a testimonial from a magistrate in Waterford alluding to his good character. He was 'honest, sober and quiet, a very willing workman'. He was also 'a good father and a loving husband'.

*Slattocks, opposite the* Hopwood Arms. Rochdale Local Studies Library collection

John Brennan sailed from Dublin on 30 April 1866 and passed through Liverpool and Manchester, looking for work as a farm-labourer. He had originally intended travelling south, but arrived in Rochdale in the sunshine early on the morning of 20 May and decided to stay.

On the stretch of turnpike road between Rochdale and Middleton was, and still is, a pub called the *Hopwood Arms Hotel.* The Rochdale Canal flows past the back door of the inn and on that sunny morning in May, with the fields and moors stretching into the distance, it must have looked idyllic. There was a smallholding attached to the pub so Brennan decided to offer his services to the landlord as an outdoor labourer.

His references were of little use here as the landlord Robert Burrows could not read. Nevertheless, he offered Brennan some casual work and the Irishman was able to find lodgings at the nearby *George and Dragon Inn.* The landlady described Brennan 'as being of above average height, stocky and with a dark complexion and white hair that gave him the appearance of an older man'.

When he walked into the *Hopwood Arms* to meet his new employer, Brennan found that the Burrows were an unusually large family, consisting of Robert Burrows, his wife Emma, their nine daughters and one son, James.

James Burrows was just eighteen but looked younger. He was 'five feet seven inches tall; slim with brown hair and grey eyes. His voice was high and somewhat effeminate.' Burrows had hardly attended school, being required to work on the farm from an early age, and like his father he was virtually illiterate. He was not renowned as a hard worker, 'preferring to spend his time in the pubs and hostelries in Slattocks and Rochdale'. He had, however, won widespread respect because of an incident that had occurred in May the previous year.

Simon Chadwick, a farm boy, had been leading a cow on a halter along the canal towpath to an adjacent field when suddenly the Rochdale Hunt in full flight, bugles blaring and hounds baying, galloped across his path. The cow panicked, leapt into the canal, dragging Simon Chadwick in after it, and swam some 30 yards with the boy in tow.

James Burrows who was on the other bank with two of his sisters, dived into the water, grabbed the boy's collar and towed him to the canal bank. He pulled himself out and lifted the boy gently from the water into the arms of his sisters; he then went along the bank and, with his father's help, hauled out the terrified cow. Boy and cow both survived.

James Burrows had enjoyed many a free beer on the strength of that piece of bravery. Twelve months on, however, and the well of goodwill had dried up. The hard-drinking Burrows was expected to pay for his pleasures.

Although the weather was warm and Burrows was thirsty and bad tempered, what provoked him to behave as he did on Monday 21 May 1866 was never satisfactorily explained. He was, however, far from happy when his father asked him to fetch a horse from the field adjoining the *Jolly Waggoner's Inn* and clean up the stables. He got the horse into the field all right, but the lure of the *Jolly Waggoner's* was too strong and, once having succumbed to temptation, there he stayed until 12pm, when he spotted a friend, Henry Clegg, on the road and went out to speak to him.

Clegg, a barman at the *George and Dragon,* had been given the afternoon off and was heading into Rochdale for a tour of the market pubs. Burrows said he would join him but he hadn't completed his chores for his father – neither did he have any money. Seeing the new Irish labourer coming down the lane, Burrows thought he had found the solution to both his problems.

James Burrows approached John Brennan and told the Irishman to take the horse into the stable then the two joined Henry Clegg and walked back towards the *Hopwood Arms.* As Brennan reached the stable, Burrows whispered to Clegg, 'I have borrowed half a crown from this old bugger this morning and I have given it him back. Now I shall have half a sovereign from him and go into Rochdale.' He followed Brennan into the stable and shut the door, leaving Clegg waiting restlessly outside.

After quarter of an hour an impatient Henry Clegg was about to abandon his friend and ride into Rochdale alone when James Burrows finally opened the stable door and closed it carefully behind him. 'Have you got it'? Clegg asked. 'I've got nothing off the bugger,' replied Burrows, 'I shall leave him in there.'

The two then decided against a trip into Rochdale and went instead to the *Jolly Waggoner's.* Alice Chatburn, the landlady, noticed that Burrows' collar was undone and his white calico shirt had dark marks on it. He went into the wash-house and came out a few minutes later with his face, hands and shirt dripping with water. He walked into the taproom and sat down next to Henry Clegg and a man called James Taylor.

Taylor was a hard man better known locally as 'Germany' because he had once fled to Bavaria to escape the English police.

Burrows whispered something to Taylor, winked at him, and then challenged him to go outside for a fist fight. Taylor had his right arm in a sling, the result of a street brawl in Rochdale, but followed Burrows out of the door, accompanied by Henry Clegg.

James Burrows stood with his arms by his side and allowed Taylor to thump him on the nose with his good hand. Burrows staggered back, blood dripping from his nose on to his shirt and the three men walked back into the pub. Henry Clegg later described it as 'the worst fight I have ever seen'.

Alice Chatburn, however, noticed that the original marks on Burrows' shirt had now been covered by fresh blood. At that point the door of the pub flew open and Alice Burrows came running in screaming for her brother.

Two hours earlier, Robert Burrows had been serving a customer in the *Hopwood Arms* when, looking up, he saw his horse wandering unattended down the turnpike road. 'Alice!' he shouted, 'get Mary to finish in here and you come with me. That idle brother of yours has let the horse loose.' The two ran into the road, Robert Burrows grabbed the horse by the mane and led him to the stable door. Alice opened the door, to be confronted by a terrible sight.

There, on the floor, partly covered with straw, was the body of the Irishman, John Brennan. Both Alice and Robert Burrows came to the conclusion that Brennan had been kicked by the horse, but it would still be necessary to call the police as well as a doctor.

Confusion reigned because nobody knew in which police division Slattocks was located. Robert Burrows went first to Middleton, to be told by the constable there that he wasn't sure, but he didn't think Slattocks was his responsibility.

After a few telegrams were despatched, the task was allotted to the Bury Constabulary and two hot and tired constables from Birch arrived on the scene at around 3.30pm. One of the officers, Isaiah Stott, was not convinced that the wounds had been inflicted by a horse. 'Not only,' he said, 'did poor Brennan look as though he had been run over by a railway train, there had clearly been several blows struck.'

Constable Stott sent for two duty sergeants, Simpson and Hardisty, who were stationed at Heywood and who arrived shortly afterwards. The two agreed that the Irishman's death was unlikely to have been caused by a horse and immediately began searching for a murder weapon.

When Alice Burrows came running into the *Jolly Waggoner*

*Constables arrived from Birch to investigate the murder.*
Rochdale Local Studies Library collection

shouting, 'Jim, the horse has killed the Irishman.' Her brother, 'turned as pale as death and said to Henry Clegg, "I shall go and see what they're saying."' (Subsequent trial testimony, as reported by the *Rochadale Observer*.) He left the pub, but within ten minutes he was back. Clegg had gone, but James Taylor was still sitting in the taproom. Burrows joined him, saying, 'They think it is murder and I think I'm for it.' Taylor asked Burrows if he had killed the Irishmen and Burrows replied: 'Aye, I did it with a crowbar, caved his skull in. I asked Irish Johnny for half a sovereign but he wouldn't give me nothing, so I let him have it.'

'That's a hanging job,' said Taylor. 'What did you do with the bar?'

'Left it in the stable,' said Burrows.

'I'd have moved it, thrown it in the canal. If you don't go and do it now, they've got you. They'll be here in five minutes.'

It took a little longer than that for the police to come for James Burrows. Frederick Booth, the doctor, had arrived at the murder scene and was sharing his expertise with the police. John Brennan, he said, 'had received five heavy blows to the head which caused deep wounds and sent splinters of bone through the brain membrane. The skull fractures had been inflicted by a heavy blunt instrument wielded with great force.'

On the night of Monday 21 May, James Burrows did not return to the *Hopwood Arms*. He and James Taylor slept in a hayloft. Isabella, one of Burrows' sisters saw him on the Tuesday morning, crossing the turnpike road. She shouted through the window that the police wanted to know his whereabouts on the previous afternoon. Burrows replied that he would be back in ten minutes and crossed the road in the direction of Thornham.

The search was on. Burrows hid around Thornham Lane during the day, returning alone to the hayloft that night. On the Wednesday morning, a Constable Shaw was poking with a pitchfork in the loft when 'he encountered something wedged in a cavity between the haymow and the wall'. That something moved and when Shaw prodded again, 'the prisoner's head emerged, all covered in straw'.

The evidence was piling up against Burrows. A bloodstained crowbar had been found in the stable and his trousers 'were seen to be well splashed with blood'. He was duly charged with, 'wilful murder' and was expected to appear before the coroner's jury at the inquest held in the *Queen Anne Hotel* in Heywood.

In the event, the shambolic inquest was mainly remarkable for the non-appearance of the prisoner. The administrative anomaly that located Slattocks in the Bury Police Division meant that the Bury magistrates were responsible for the prisoner and they wouldn't allow him to travel to Heywood, especially not to a pub.

The Deputy Coroner was appalled. It meant that evidence against the prisoner would be presented but that Burrows would not be able to defend himself. He rounded on the senior police officer, Superintendent Milne, saying, 'it was a monstrous nonsense that the prisoner should not be before them because they met in a pub. How many hundreds of inquests,' he demanded, 'were held in pubs?' Milne held his ground, replying that he did not know the number, but that the practise should be stopped. 'That is not for you to decide!' thundered the outraged Deputy Coroner.

It may not have been usual to bar the accused from the inquest, but in truth it would have made little difference had Burrows been present. The medical evidence and witness statements were damning and Burrows was committed for trial at the next session of the Manchester Assizes.

The trial was also a formality. James Burrows had failed to impress the warders by 'singing, dancing and capering in his cell' and a procession of witnesses spoke of his, 'coarse and vulgar habits' and his 'inappropriate behaviour and tendency to acts of violence'.

Queen Anne Hotel, *Heywood – venue for the inquest.*
Rochdale Local Studies Library collection

Once the medical evidence had been presented, those present on the day of the murder were cross-examined. The Judge, Mr Justice Henshaw, warned James Taylor, who had described how he had advised Burrows to dispose of the murder weapon that he was in danger of 'branding himself as an accessory by his own words'.

The jury took just fifteen minutes to reach a verdict and the judge donned his black cap and pronounced the death sentence.

Burrows' execution was to take place in Manchester on 26 August 1866. Manchester was not a regular venue for hangings. It had only recently become an assize town and, prior to receiving its enhanced status, the last execution to have taken place was way back in 1798. Previously, prisoners charged with capital offences had been tried and executed at Liverpool or Lancaster.

A Manchester-based campaign was mounted to petition for Burrows' reprieve. This was motivated more by horror at the prospect of a public hanging with all the attendant hysteria, rather than any mitigating circumstances relating to the murder. However, the campaigners had to base their appeal on something, and cited the extreme youth of the condemned man and the spontaneous, non-premeditated nature of the crime, in mitigation.

The petition was circulated throughout Bury, Rochdale and Manchester, but the organizers could only raise 1,000 signatures, three of which were allegedly those of Queen Victoria.

Another problem arose from the lack of expertise the authorities in Manchester had in hosting this kind of event. For a start, there appeared to be no suitable venue to erect the scaffold. The new Manchester prison had not been completed and the New Bailey gaol in Salford would not accommodate the huge number of people expected to throng in for the spectacle. It was even proposed to approach the authorities in Liverpool to see whether the hanging could be transferred there. Manchester's civic pride would not allow that to happen and eventually it was resolved to demolish a wall running alongside the New Bailey to provide space for the predicted 30,000 spectators.

James Burrows had not endeared himself to the staff at the New Bailey: 'He indulged in displays of bravado, singing lewd songs and mocking his fellow captives.' However, suddenly he began to demonstrate both an amazing aptitude and appetite for reading. He attracted a sponsor, a sort of teacher/moral adviser, called Thomas Wright and within three weeks, from being totally illiterate, 'he could read complicated texts and write tolerably well'.

He was visited by his father, mother and each of his nine sisters and astonished them all with 'his new-found abilities'. Unfortunately, there was precious little reading time left for James Burrows.

At 10pm on Friday 25 August people began gathering in the open area to the front of the scaffold. They sang, they told jokes, they fought and they scuffled with pickpockets. 'The smell of roasting meat and bacon filled the air and hawkers and pedlars plied their trade.' By 3am most had fallen into a drunken stupor and then, 'somebody decided to speed the dawn by imitating the sound of a cockerel. This was taken up by hundreds more until the yard echoed to a deafening cacophony of crowing, braying, whinnying and mooing.'

The crowd, pushing against the barriers, booed energetically as a platoon of police tried to make their way to the scaffold and then howled even louder as a preacher attempted to clamber over the barrier. 'They hoisted their natural enemy into the air and when one part of the mob had raised him, he was passed on for another set of eager hands to lower him to the ground and in such a way was carried back to where he started from.'

At around 5am, the police tried to edge the crowd back up the street, one of the inspectors vigorously laying about him with his lead-lined truncheon. Just as the situation threatened to spiral out of control, wiser counsel prevailed and the crowd were allowed up to the first barrier, with the police positioned behind an inner fence.

A contingent of spectators arrived from Rochdale on the 6am train, 'and by virtue of their greater freshness managed to gain themselves a prime position at the front of the crowd'. Once there, 'they began to throw celery and other vegetables and a boisterous good humour prevailed'.

A figure dressed in black who clambered on to the platform was taken to be Calcraft the hangman and was greeted with renewed booing. The man, however, had been despatched by the magistrates to drape a huge black cloth over the scaffold, hiding the activities on the gallows from the crowd below. A storm of protest erupted, persuading the magistrates that from the perspective of public safety, the crowd would have to witness the event: 'They had come to see the full sight and the full sight they would see.'

An impromptu game of football with a priest's hat followed and the crowd then took to 'setting fire to handkerchiefs and scarves and throwing the blazing objects high into the air'.

Four youths clambered up the drainpipe of an adjacent warehouse and sat on a window-sill lobbing missiles into the crowd below. The magistrates ordered the police to evict them and three constables shinned up the drainpipe in pursuit. The crowd showed their appreciation by hurling 'a deafening barrage of abuse, and more vegetables at the police'. The youths 'climbed through the open window and down the stairs to freedom'. Cries of: 'What time is it?' and 'Hurry up!' reverberated around the street and at 7.50am the scaffold door opened.

James Burrows had spent a sleepless night listening to the carnival outside his cell. He had used his newly acquired skills to read from the Bible. He had confessed his crimes and was praying with the priest and Thomas Wright when Calcraft the hangman came to fasten his arms behind him. Then with the

High Sheriff of Lancashire, the Mayor of Salford and several high-ranking police officers in the lead, Burrows was taken along the corridor and into the yard to the scaffold. 'He mounted the platform with a firm tread and was led underneath the beam to the drop.'

Calcraft put the white cap over James Burrows' eyes, stepped back and pulled the bolt. 'The fall was considerable and the culprit's neck appeared to be completely dislocated. There were a few convulsive movements and the body was still.' In the custom of the day, James Burrow's body hung in full view of the crowd for an hour. When it was cut down, however, interest had faded and there just twelve people remaining in the prison yard.

In a statement written to be read out after the execution was completed James Burrows said how regretted his murderous attack on John Brennan and sent his condolences to his widow and six children.

The chaplain said that he had never encountered anyone as 'penitent and heartily sorry for his actions as James Burrows'.

Neither Burrows nor his victim were buried at home. James Burrows' body was buried at the side of the prison in Salford and John Brennan was laid to rest, far from Waterford, in the burial ground of Jericho Workhouse in Bury.

# CHAPTER 9

# Bloodbath at the Vicarage

Although Todmorden is now part of Calderdale in West Yorkshire, it was not until 1889 that half the town lost its Lancashire heritage. Prior to that the portion of Todmorden west of the river Calder was firmly in the Red Rose County, part of the Parish of Rochdale.

The name Todmorden probably means, 'the valley of Totta's marsh', although, in a popular alternative derivation, two words meaning death – the German 'Tod' and the French 'mort' – meet the Anglo-Saxon word 'den' to identify Todmorden as 'Death, Death Wood': a far more appropriate definition in the light of the following horror story.

Over the centuries, Todmorden grew to be a prosperous wool producing area, but because of its cultural links with Lancashire and Manchester, by the 1850s cotton production was overtaking that of wool and Todmorden was considered to be one of the Lancashire cotton towns.

The Rochdale influence was strong because of the role St Chad's Church played as the spiritual centre of this vast parish. Up until the 1840s, every adult resident living within the Parish of Rochdale had to pay a levy to maintain St Chad's, whether they attended the church or not. This payment was known as the Church Rate.

Todmorden people were outraged by this tax; not only did they live miles from St Chad's but many were nonconformists, Methodists, Quakers, Baptists, each with their own churches or chapels to maintain. The local protests against the Rate were led by John Fielden, a radical Todmorden millowner who was also the leader of the Ten Hours campaign for factory reform. He and two Rochdale protesters, John Bright and Thomas Livsey, spearheaded a movement that not only saw the abolition of the Church Rate in Rochdale parish, but also led to the concept being abandoned throughout the country.

However, the close ties between Todmorden and St Chad's Church were maintained. Christ Church Todmorden was in the gift of the vicars of St Chad's and most Todmorden vicars were appointees from Rochdale.

Anthony John Plow, the son of the Reverend Henry Plow of Bradley in Hampshire had moved to Rochdale in 1860 at the recommendation of the long-serving vicar of St Chad's, the

*The Reverend JEN Molesworth, mentor of the murdered vicar.*
Rochdale Local Studies Library collection

Reverend J E N Molesworth. The Reverend Molesworth
became close to Anthony Plow and was instrumental in his
move from the curacy of St James' Parish Church Rochdale to
St Chad's. Anthony Plow even married Harriet Bridges, the
daughter of Molesworth's second wife.

The Plow's happiness appeared assured when Anthony was
appointed vicar of Todmorden and then, when in February

*The Reverend Anthony Plow, victim of Miles Weatherill.*
Rochdale Local Studies Library collection

1868, Harriet Plow gave birth to their first child, a daughter, Catherine Hilda.

Reverend Plow was a familiar figure in Todmorden, not only in the pleasant green areas around the vicarage, but also in the rougher terraces and courtyards so typical of the booming cotton towns.

In one of these smoke-blackened terraces, Back Brook Street, lived Alice Weatherill. Alice was a widow. The death of her husband Richard, a man of 'violence and uncertain temper' had forced Alice to take in lodgers.

A procession of unsavoury characters passed through the house, leaving a deep but unhealthy impression on Alice's young son, Miles. Miles Weatherill displayed early signs of having inherited his father's anti-social tendencies. He was fiery tempered and prone to fighting but crucially he also possessed 'a lively intelligence and an enquiring mind'. Consequently, although he was sent out to work as a weaver at the age of twelve, he developed a passion for learning.

Miles would read to his mother and younger sister. He frequented the book shops and reading rooms until his enthusiasm and 'a remarkable ability to pass on his learning' made him an obvious candidate for the role of teacher at Christ Church Sunday school.

Weatherill was well turned-out, fit and active and made a good impression on those around him, including, at first, the vicar. Gradually, however, Anthony Plow began to have reservations about Miles Weatherill.

The vicarage at Todmorden was a lively place. Harriet Plow was pregnant and the vicar's salary was generous enough to enable him to employ a number of servants to support himself and his soon to be expanded family. Amongst these were cook Sarah Elizabeth Bell, servants Elizabeth Spink and Mary Hodgson and Jane Smith who acted as a 'maid-of-all-work'.

*Miles Weatherill, the vicarage murderer.* Rochdale Local Studies Library collection

Sarah Bell was only sixteen years old. She was from York and had come to Todmorden on the recommendation of a cleric from York Minster. Because of her youth, Anthony Plow had given assurances to her family that the girl would be under his protection and he would act, 'in loco parentis' while Sarah was in his service.

By June 1867 Miles Weatherill had become a frequent visitor to the vicarage and had fallen for Sarah. He had read about courting protocol and knew that it would be necessary 'to seek permission from the vicar in order to woo her'. Anthony Plow's reservations concerning Weatherill now surfaced publicly. There had been stories circulating concerning Weatherill's 'wild and unpredictable behaviour at work' and Plow told him 'in no uncertain terms, that the girl was too young and that he should not think of pursuing her'.

In order to ensure that no meetings should take place between the two, Plow restricted Sarah's movements, confining her on her day off to the vicarage, under his wife's supervision.

Plow could hardly physically restrain his charge, however, and inevitably Sarah was able to sneak out of the vicarage for clandestine meetings with Miles Weatherill. She would return from these assignations 'flushed and excited' and was unable to resist sharing her adventures with the maid Jane Smith. In turn, Jane Smith could not resist sharing the secret with Harriet Plow, who was then obliged then to tell her husband.

Reverend Plow was furious. He consulted with the Reverend Molesworth at Rochdale and on 1 November 1867 decided that if he was unable to control Sarah, then he had no alternative but to send her back to York.

Miles Weatherill was devastated by Sarah's sudden departure. He wrote regularly to her in York, begging her to return to Todmorden, but although she responded cordially enough to his increasingly desperate letters, Sarah refused.

On 26 February, Weatherill boarded the train for York determined to persuade Sarah to quit her new job in York and come back with him to Todmorden. Again she declined, but for the first time she did reveal to Weatherill the circumstances behind her leaving. When he heard that it was Jane Smith who had alerted the Plows to the furtive romance, Weatherill was livid. On Monday 2 March, returning alone on the Todmorden train, he plotted a terrible revenge.

Miles Weatherill drank with friends until ten o'clock that evening but was 'as sober at the end of the night as he was at the

*Sarah Bell – the inspiration for Miles Weatherill's killing spree.*
Rochdale Local Studies Library collection

beginning'. He had a further whisky in the *Black Swan*, 'went back home for some special items of equipment', and set off for the vicarage.

When he left his house that night Weatherill was indeed well-equipped . . . for murder. Around his waist was a leather belt that he had adapted to accommodate a hatchet, four pistols and some strong twine. All the guns were primed with caps and shot.

At the side of the vicarage was the scullery. Weatherill crept through the bushes, unravelled the twine from his belt and to prevent any escape from the house, tied the door handle firmly to a drainpipe He then moved stealthily to the back door and repeated the process. Inside, however, Jane Smith had heard a series of scraping noises and alerted Anthony Plow who ran out of the front door to investigate. He bumped into Miles Weatherill who was rounding the corner to make his entrance.

*Jane Smith – victim of Miles Weatherill.* Rochdale Local Studies Library collection

Plow dived at the intruder and as they wrestled together, Weatherill pulled a pistol from his belt, aimed at the vicar and pulled the trigger. The hammer stuck, the gun failed to fire twice and a furious Weatherill wrenched the hatchet from his belt and began to lash out at Plow, chopping through his jacket into his arm and catching him a sickening blow to the head.

The two reeled through the door and into the house. Elizabeth Spink, servant to Harriet Plow, grabbed Weatherill by the hair and yanked him backwards. Whispering repeatedly, 'Be quiet, be quiet,' she managed to ward off his blows until 'she felt that she had succeeded in calming the man down'.

Unfortunately Jane Smith walked into the room at this point and Weatherill, seeing the cause of all his tribulations in front of him, dropped the useless gun and launched himself at her, hatchet in hand. Weatherill landed a series of brutal blows to the servant's head and, streaming with blood, Jane Smith crashed against the dining room door, which swung open under her weight. She fell through the doorway, somehow managing to push the door shut behind her.

In taking a final swipe at the girl, Weatherill lost his grip on the hatchet and it flew spiralling to the floor. The fourth servant Mary Hodgson, who had joined the melee, kicked the hatchet along the floor out of Weatherill's reach and picked it up.

Anthony Plow, who had grabbed the pistol, stared in horrified disbelief as Weatherill, no more than 2 feet away, drew a second gun from his belt.

Again Plow charged forward, searing pain from the hatchet wounds shooting through his right arm as he clattered into his attacker. And again he managed to disarm Weatherill, scooping the gun from his hand and forcing him against the wall.

Surely, he must have thought, they were safe now. Plow raced out of the front door and across to Well Lane and the home of William Greenwood the church organist.

Elizabeth Spink was still attempting to calm Weatherill, but the intruder was beyond reason . . . and armed to the teeth. He hurled the servant to the floor and, his third pistol in hand, went in search of his quarry.

Jane Smith did not have the strength to crawl to safety. She lay in the dining room, slumped against the table. Weatherill kicked open the door and shot her from close range. There was nothing now for Elizabeth Spink to do but run for help. Weatherill continued his rampage. Upstairs were Harriet Plow (in bed with her month-old baby) and her nurse, Margaret Ball.

The racket downstairs had wakened the baby. Margaret Ball went to investigate and, standing halfway up the stairs, was horrified to witness the assassination of Jane Smith in the dining room below. Then, even worse, she saw Miles Weatherill clean and reload his pistol and with slow deliberation, begin his ascent of the stairs, the pistol in one hand and a poker in the other.

Margaret Ball rushed along the landing, ran into Harriet Plow's bedroom, slammed the door behind her, put her back against it and dug her feet into the carpet. Weatherill flung himself against the door and forced it open. Margaret Ball was not the target of his anger and she managed to squeeze past him, run downstairs and join the procession leaving the vicarage to seek assistance.

Miles Weatherill leaned across the bed, picked up the baby in its cradle and put it on the floor. Then he shot twice through the bedclothes. Harriet Plow, struggling out of bed and begging Weatherill not to hurt the baby, became wedged between the heavy bed and the wall and Weatherill set about her with the poker, battering her insensible.

Suddenly the house was alive with people including several police officers, although it was parish clerk, George Stansfield, who entered the bedroom, took a trembling Miles Weatherill by the arm and led him quietly downstairs.

Weatherill's fury was spent. Head bowed, he walked with a constable to the lock-up at the bottom of Ferney Lea.

The vicarage was a scene of devastation. Local GP, Dr Cockcroft ministered as well as he could to the Plows. Anthony Plow stood 'like a man in at trance'. Harriet Plow had such severe wounds to her head that she was breathing through a flap of torn skin on her ruined nose. She was taken from the house, without her baby, to stay with another member of the Molesworth family, George, the Deputy Coroner.

Jane Smith was beyond help, killed outright by the bullet from Weatherill's pistol; she was buried at Christ Church the very next day.

Superintendent Pickering from the Rochdale Constabulary was sent for and the inquest examination was held at the *Black Swan* in front of magistrates John and Joshua Fielden and Abraham Ormerod on Friday 6 March. All the surviving victims of that terrible ordeal, with the exception of Harriet Plow, gave evidence. The Reverend Anthony Plow appeared 'dignified and confident'.

Within a week he was dead.

He died, according to the inquest verdict, from 'an inflammation of the brain, caused by a blow from a heavy instrument, the victim of a murderous attack by Miles Weatherill'.

Although, as far as anyone could make out, the baby Catherine Hilda Plow was not the victim of a physical attack by Weatherill, she died on the same day as her father.

A terrible series of funerals followed culminating on Saturday 14 March, with the body of Anthony Plow lying in state and with Reverend J E N Molesworth leading scores of clergymen in a vigil beside the coffin.

So infamous was the crime that Queen Victoria sent Harriet Plow a message in her own hand expressing her 'deepest condolence and sympathy'.

Miles Weatherill was committed for trial at Manchester Assizes on 28 March 1868.

The judge began the proceedings in Manchester by awarding Elizabeth Spink £5 and Mary Hodgson £2, 10 shillings for their bravery in attempting to protect the Plows. However, what caused the biggest stir that day, receiving frenzied coverage in the Manchester press, was the appearance in court of the subject of Weatherill's affection, Sarah Elizabeth Bell.

Dressed in black, she wore a veil throughout the proceedings and 'casting her eyes down, she never so much as glanced at the prisoner'.

Inevitably, after deliberating for only six minutes, the jury returned a guilty verdict and the judge donning his black cap, pronounced that Weatherill 'would hang by the neck until he was dead'.

There was much speculation in Todmorden that insanity ran in Weatherill's family ('His father a crazed and raving man and his mother and sister little better than idiots') and that had this been revealed to the jury, they may have been moved to recommend clemency.

This view did not find many takers, however, as Weatherill repeatedly 'refused to repent his sins'. He even boasted to John Dawson – preacher and magistrate, who visited him in his condemned cell – that he would 'open Jane Smith's secret to the whole of Todmorden'. This 'secret' turned out to be that Jane had given birth to an illegitimate child, a revelation that paled into insignificance beside the horror of Weatherill's bloodbath. However, in a letter to a friend written a week before the date set for his hanging, Weatherill finally, if reluctantly, acknowledged his guilt:

*Dear Friend,*

*I thought I would write a few lines to you as you have been so kind. I suppose you know I have been found guilty, and that I shall have to be hung. It is an awful and shameful death to die, but I have deserved it and there is no chance left. I was very sorry when I heard that Mr Plow and the babe were dead. Oh! I hope there will be no more to die; it is so terrible to think of. I wish he had given me the privilege of keeping company with Sarah. I would not have cared for going into the house if he had only let her have her Sunday outs, but he would not, and oh, what has it come to. If he had given me the chance, what a different man I should have been. I should have been a teacher in the Sunday School, a communicant in the Church, and if I had once more taken of that Holy feast, it would have been a heavenly feast to my soul, for I would not have taken that Holy Communion in mockery as a cloak to make people think I was good. No, I should have taken an interest in doing what good I could for the school and church, and in the long run he would have found me a useful man. And what a comfort I should have been to my poor mother and sister and how happy my Sarah would have been. We did not want to get married just then, but I would have married her before she left Todmorden had she been willing. No, I wanted to get a better trade and make a little more money than I had. Then I would have married her and been happy with her, but when she left Todmorden, there was a turning point in me. Yes, I turned wild; I cared little what I did. I spent all my money, I saw nothing but poverty and despair and now I am condemned to die. Ah I was a changed man when she left, ah, I am sorry to say, changed for the worse. I shall soon be parted from her for ever in this world but I will try to meet her in heaven, but there is only poor signs yet of me, for my heart is yet hardened, but I will try to die a true penitent. See you live for another and better world for Christ has died to save us all, and may we all meet in heaven.*

*From yours sincerely*
*Miles Weatherill*

*PS. You can do as you like with this letter, I will find no fault with you if you publish it. I am not ashamed.*

*Harriet and baby Catherine Hilda Plow – victims of Miles Weatherill.*
Rochdale Local Studies Library collection

The date for the hanging was Saturday 4 April 1868. The *Manchester Examiner* captured the tone of the proceedings on the morning of the execution.

*A good staff of police was in attendance, and the arrangements were such as to suppress any disturbance that might arise, but no interference was necessary. To have attempted to stop the ribald and disgusting behaviour, such as is customarily exhibited at public executions would have led to consequences of a by no means pleasant character, and the populace were allowed to indulge in the full flow of their spirits, coarse and vulgar as they were. Some of the popular songs of the day, mingled with jokes and attempted witticisms were the prevailing source of amusement.*

This was the last public hanging to take place in the North of England and the spectators were making the most of it. The scaffold had been erected early and by 7am 'the crowd had swollen to 10,000 people'.

Miles Weatherill had not slept during the night and when the prison chaplain arrived 'he was tired but expressed sadness for what he had done'.

The hangman, William Calcraft, came next to tie the prisoner's arms and was impressed with Weatherill's 'dignity, nerve and resolution'. They set off in a procession, leaving the condemned cell and reaching the scaffold 'as the prison bell tolled the hour of eight'.

A great roar went up from the crowd as Weatherill followed Timothy Flaherty, a child murderer from Droylsden, up the wooden steps. He climbed without hesitation to the platform, a prayer book in his hand.

He waited as the death penalty was carried out on Flaherty, and then moved forward, saying to his captors, 'Don't hold me, I can stand by myself.' Then a white cap was placed over his head and the noose dropped around his neck and within ten seconds Miles Weatherill's ordeal was over.

Harriet Plow's ordeal lasted a little, but not much, longer. The experience devastated her; she never recovered and died in Berkshire on 19 March 1869, almost a year to the day after the burial of her husband and daughter.

In the manner of the time, the murders and their shocking aftermath were recounted in a broadsheet that was sold by the thousand on the streets of Manchester, Rochdale and Todmorden. It was entitled: 'Miles Weatherill, the Young Weaver and his Sweetheart, Sarah Bell'.

CHAPTER **10**

# Poor Annie's Ghost

**I**n July 1882 the whole of Dawson Square in the Mount Pleasant area of Rochdale stood empty. According to the *Rochdale Times*, the houses had been abandoned because residents were convinced that the courtyard was haunted. In February 1877, neighbours had witnessed 'a murderous assault' on Annie McKenna and had done nothing. Now their consciences were plaguing them. 'Poor Annie' or, more likely, her vengeful spirit, had returned.

The area known as Mount Pleasant was a rectangular plot of land overlooking Whitworth Road; some 300 yards long and 200 yards wide, 'the Mount' was crammed with terraces, tenements and courtyards. The development had been constructed in the 1830s to provide accommodation for the workers at Joseph Bright's Fieldhead Mill. The houses were cold, damp and infested. All the 'night soil', rubbish and slops were thrown into the unpaved alleys to mingle with the scum in stagnant puddles. 'In the winter it stank; in the summer it stank even worse.'

The Mount was home to some 1,500 people, many of them itinerant travellers, most of them Irish and all of them poor. Few stayed because they wanted to but most made the best of it and Saturday night was the time when the frustrations of the week came pouring out and when personal demons were exorcised. There was dancing, drinking and fighting, but any violence was normally contained and the police tended to stay away 'and let them get on with it'.

The McKennas were, on the surface no different from most. Annie was young and pretty, 'about 24 as far as her mother could judge', with jet-black hair and blue eyes. She had lived in England for sixteen years, yet still retained an Irish lilt to her voice. Her mother, who had brought all three of her daughters from Ireland, had settled first in Liverpool. There, Annie had met John McKenna and they were married in 1871.

John McKenna was, by common consent, wild. He was Irish,

about the same age as his wife: 'A tall, broad, good-looking man, with a nose bent from fighting and a liking for strong drink.' He had been in some trouble with the law, but nothing serious and all related to drinking or brawling. He was a plasterer by trade and considered a reliable worker. The McKennas lived on Dawson Square in a one-up, one-down property, built directly on to the courtyard.

On Sundays, while his wife and mother-in-law attended church, John McKenna would meet with a group of men and walk to the hills above Whitworth. Here he would engage in a pastime variously known as 'kicking', 'punsing' or 'clogging'.

This 'sport' had been common in the Rochdale area for over a century but was now outlawed. A group of spectators would form a circle and two men would enter the 'ring', sometimes naked, more usually stripped to the waist, wearing a pair of clogs; then, egged on by the crowd, the contestants would kick each other, 'from ankle to upper body until one either yielded or passed out'. Betting on the outcome was a potential source of extra drinking money for the weekend.

Curiously, the all-time champion of these contests was: 'a man of some breeding, Benjamin Healey, a Whitworth surveyor'. However, John McKenna – who 'never wore clogs in the street, preferring stout shoes' – was considered to be 'a fine kicker' and often returned home with a cache of prize money.

The McKennas had two children: the elder five and the younger three years old.

Annie McKenna worked in the weaving shed at Ashworth's cotton mill. She was pregnant, but had received no support in the home since her mother, who had lived with the McKennas, had been thrown out by John McKenna. Her mother had moved in with Annie's sister in Heywood and visited Rochdale infrequently.

It was Saturday 24 February 1877, a cold, damp afternoon and John McKenna had been drinking. There was nothing unusual in that but by 3pm, sitting in the *Coach and Horses* with friends, he had become morose. He said that he had seen his wife pass the pub window with another man; an event that had been witnessed by no one else in his group.

At 4pm, John McKenna returned home with three strangers he had met in the pub: a man, his wife and their son. He sent Annie McKenna out for 'some quarts of beer'. The two adults and John McKenna between them finished off the beer and at 5.30pm the visitors left.

Annie McKenna was concerned. She had drunk nothing, while her husband and his new friends had drunk themselves virtually insensible and now, with just the two of them in the house, John McKenna was becoming abusive. Annie knew from bitter experience that his threats of violence invariably became a reality; she had the bruises to prove it.

McKenna suddenly began shouting. He had, he said, seen Annie on Yorkshire Street with another man. He stood unsteadily out of his chair and began to move towards his wife. Then he started yawning; he slumped back into the chair, his head dropped and he was asleep.

Dawson Square had two small gas lamps emitting a flickering light. The gas mantles in the houses were brighter and through the gloom, Annie McKenna could see her neighbour Mary Higgins, clearing the tea table in the house opposite.

Annie was in a dilemma. She was desperate to leave the house and talk to her neighbour. On the other hand, if she went across the courtyard to see Mary Higgins and John McKenna woke up with no tea on the table, he would have another excuse for violence.

Eventually, Annie McKenna decided she could stay in the same room as her snoring husband no longer and crept across the unpaved yard to her neighbour. She talked to Mary Higgins for about three-quarters of an hour and then, at around 6.45pm, jumped to her feet saying, 'he will kill me if I don't have his tea on the table'.

Annie's worst fears were realized. Her husband was sitting at the table with his head in his hands. He looked up when she came through the door and said, 'where's my bloody tea?'

Mary Higgins was not surprised when, at 8.15pm, Annie McKenna ran back across the yard in tears. She said, 'He's upstairs, gone mad; he doesn't know I'm out.'

Annie sat down, but two minutes later John McKenna burst through the door shouting: 'Is my bloody wife here?' Mary Higgins raised her shawl to hide Annie and in the half-light McKenna didn't see her. Mary asked McKenna to sit down and suggested that she buy half a gallon of beer for him. But John McKenna had spotted his wife in the shadows. 'You bloody cow! Get out! I'll pay you for this when we get outside!' he roared. At that point, Mary Higgins' husband Joseph arrived home from work and he too offered to get some beer. 'We can have a quart and talk, Jack.' McKenna grabbed Annie by the hair. 'For God's sake Jack, calm down and have some sense,' said

*'Two small gas lamps emitting a flickring light.'* Rochdale Local Studies Library collection

Joseph Higgins, but he did nothing to intervene as McKenna dragged Annie back across the courtyard.

Unusually, the McKenna's elder child was with his grandmother in Heywood, but Mary Higgins noticed that Annie had her three-year-old daughter by the hand as the door slammed shut behind her.

Mary Higgins hurried after the McKennas and tried to open their door, but it was locked. She looked through the window. Annie McKenna was sitting on the bed with her husband standing over her. Suddenly he struck her brutally over the eye with his fist. Annie's head flew sideways and hit the mantelpiece with a sickening crack.

She fell over the fireplace into the fire-irons with her legs twisted beneath her. John McKenna began 'kicking her viciously in the face and head for nearly five minutes'. Annie was screaming: 'Jack, don't kill me!' and 'Murder!'. Outside Mary Higgins was shouting 'Murder!' as well, but no one came to help.

Mary Higgins ran three doors down to fetch Susan Whelan and the two hurried back to the McKenna's. The door was open. John McKenna was demanding that his wife get up and when she didn't, he kicked her in the head. Susan Whelan lifted a table that had fallen across the doorway and said: 'Don't kill her John. Why do you want to kill her?'

McKenna's reply was to scream: 'What's that table got to do with you? Get out of my house! This is not your affair.'

The two women left as McKenna began pulling his wife across the floor. They did not raise the alarm.

Henry Dunn, an acquaintance of John McKenna, came to the house at about 9.15pm. He too had been drinking. He walked in the room and there, next to the slop-stone, Annie McKenna lay motionless on the floor. Towering over her was John McKenna with a bucket of water in his hands. He heaved the contents over his wife, and then when she didn't move, he kicked her again in the face.

Henry Dunn caught John McKenna's arm and said: 'You'll not do that again.'

McKenna swung a punch at Dunn, missed and Dunn charged forward, knocking McKenna to the floor. The two men traded blows, McKenna 'spitting teeth from his mouth'. The pair struggled to their feet and 'punched and kicked each other around the room, until they fell out of the front door into the mud'.

The fight continued for some ten minutes; then, still drunk but now battered black and blue, Henry Dunn abandoned his

*'Cold, damp and infested with vermin.'* Rochdale Local Studies Library collection

rescue attempt and staggered away.

John McKenna crossed the courtyard and walked home.

Another neighbour, Thomas O'Day, entered the McKenna's house at about 9.45pm. Annie McKenna was on the bed soaking wet and semi-conscious, 'making no noise except a moaning'. O'Day said: 'What's to do?' and John McKenna, who had his three-year-old daughter on his knee said: 'We've had a bit of bother.'

McKenna put the child down, went to the bed, put his left hand under the pillow, levered his wife up and punched her in the face.

O'Day said, 'Jack, you've done enough.' McKenna reached into his pocket, pulled out a shilling and told O'Day to get some more beer. O'Day meekly left the house, returning five minutes later with a full jug. Annie McKenna had stopped moaning. O'Day went to the bed and put his head to her chest. 'Jack,' he said, 'she's dead.'

'She's not,' said McKenna. He didn't move.

O'Day reluctantly went in search of a police officer, a task that took him over an hour.

By the time O'Day had located Constable Dyer on Yorkshire Street and the pair had returned to Dawson Square, a doctor had been called to the house, but there was nothing he could do for Annie McKenna. There was no sign of life. Neither was there any sign of her husband.

Thanks to Thomas O'Day, McKenna had over an hour's start on his pursuers. It was perfectly possible for police in their Town Hall HQ to send messages, descriptions and even whole wanted notices to Manchester, Liverpool or London via telegram, but they had no mechanical means of contacting their own constables walking their beats around the town.

When he was informed of McKenna's escape, the best Superintendent Milne could do was to round up half a dozen runners and send them zigzagging across Rochdale, armed with a description of the suspect in the hope of intercepting a constable. Unsurprisingly, McKenna slipped through this ineffective cordon.

Superintendent Milne interviewed the witnesses to the assault, 'regardless of the hour or their state of sobriety', and gleaned that McKenna had brothers in both Liverpool and Glasgow. Milne briefed his detectives and despatched Detective Sergeant Banks to track the suspect down.

Banks was an inspired choice. He was dogged, but crucially, intelligent and resourceful. Conscious that he was not receiving any sightings of McKenna at the railway stations, he established roadblocks and came to the conclusion that, incredibly, McKenna was walking to Liverpool over the fields. McKenna eluded two agents at Bolton and Sergeant Banks resolved to wait for the suspect outside his brother's house in Wavertree.

A day went by and there was no sign of McKenna, so on a hunch, Banks caught an omnibus and sat on the wall next to the harbour booking office of the Glasgow Packet Steamers. Just ten minutes later, John McKenna walked along the waterfront and joined the queue at the booking office. Sergeant Banks put his hand on McKenna's shoulder and said, 'I want you for killing your wife on Saturday.' 'Oh heavens!' said McKenna and burst into tears.

The post-mortem on the body of Annie McKenna at Dawson's Square was traumatic for all concerned. Annie's mother and sister would not let the body go, 'kissing the face of the deceased and wailing all the while'. When Annie's mother was told what a post-mortem entailed, 'she flung herself over her daughter's body and had to be dragged away screaming'.

*The Rochdale detective squad in 1877.* Greater Manchester Police Museum

The prisoner was brought back to Rochdale, but not by a direct route. Fearing a riot, Superintendent Milne had placed a number of officers as decoys at Rochdale railway station and had re-routed Detective Sergeant Banks and John McKenna to Bury. However half the population of Bury appeared to have been alerted and at Knowsley Street 'the prisoner was met by over 3,000 people baying for his blood'. McKenna was bundled into a police wagon and 'with three horses flanking, the convoy galloped into Rochdale'.

The inquest was held in Rochdale Town Hall. McKenna was the first suspected murderer to be brought from the police cells and up the spiral staircase into the new police court.

A procession of witnesses took the stand and the jury expressed 'considerable surprise' that so many had visited the scene of the crime without managing to prevent the tragedy. Then the room fell quiet as Dr Colley March presented his evidence:

*The face of the deceased was covered in bruises, scratches and abrasions. The right eyebrow and cheek were badly bruised. Both lips were cut internally and the lower lip was divided. The lower jaw was bruised and the neck was bruised as if grabbed by a hand. The head was uniformly swollen. The body was universally bruised from neck to ankle. There were contused wounds over the body and the backs of both hands were covered in bruises and contusions. The whole surface of the scalp was covered with effused blood. All the corresponding tissues of the scalp were pulpified. There was a fracture of the skull at the front and rear. The baby too was lost in the tragedy.*

The doctor concluded it was unlikely that 'any one single blow had killed Annie McKenna, although any number could have been potentially fatal'.

The jury retired at the Coroner's instructions, 'without fire or food until they reached a verdict', which would not have caused much discomfort as 'they were back within a minute'. The prisoner was told to stand while the foreman gave the jury's decision: 'Guilty of Wilful Murder'. The Coroner asked if McKenna had anything to say and 'to loud hissing and booing from the public gallery' the prisoner replied that he and his wife had 'both been drunk and had argued as a result'. McKenna was ordered to stand trial at the spring session of Manchester Assizes.

John McKenna hardly ate between then and the hearing in Manchester on 3 March. However, he seemed confident that he would not be found guilty of 'Wilful Murder' and 'if given the opportunity, would admit to the lesser charge of manslaughter'.

Hundreds of people from Rochdale travelled to Manchester on the 8.30am train and were waiting impatiently in the court at ten o'clock when the prisoner was brought up from the cells.

In front of the judge, Mr Justice Manisty, McKenna pleaded not guilty to the murder charge and the prosecution 'presented a case of pure unmitigated, brutal circumstance', calling Mary Higgins, Joseph Higgins, Susan Whelan, Henry Dunn, and Thomas O'Day as principal witnesses.

On the following morning it was the turn of Counsel for the Defence, Robert Blair. Blair conceded that the fatal attacks had been perpetrated by John McKenna and that 'the severity and brutality of the crime were undeniable, but,' he argued, 'nothing the prosecution offered proved pre-meditation. In a strange way,' he added, 'the fact that Mr McKenna poured water over his wife and then kicked her to wake her up, indicated that he had not believed her dead or had intended to kill her. Indeed, as Mr O'Day has revealed to us, the defendant was convinced at the end of his assault, that his wife still lived.'

Blair, summing up, said: 'It is thankfully rare that the best a defender can say about a client is that he is not a murderer; yet,' he concluded, 'that is what I say to you now.'

Mr Justice Manisty took the opportunity to censure Annie McKenna's neighbours, 'for allowing such a terrible tragedy to occur without raising the alarm,' then he turned to the jury.

To his surprise, and the defendant's horror, the jury declined to retire to consider their verdict. 'Have you already reached a conclusion on the charge of Wilful Murder?' asked the Judge. 'We have Your Honour,' replied the foreman: 'Guilty'.

McKenna was asked if there was anything he could say which would allow the Judge not to pass the maximum sentence allowed by law. In a barely audible voice McKenna replied: 'Nothing.'

A black cap was placed on Mr Justice Manisty's head by an attendant and he addressed the prisoner:

*I will not dwell on this case, I have done so once and I do not intend to do so again. You are a sad, sad instance of the conse-*

*quences of over indulgence in drink . . . If that wretched vice is*
*continued on any longer to the extent it is now, I am afraid*
*there will be many more in your current wretched condition. I*
*hope this will discourage others from taking the same route as*
*yourself, but I will not inflict more pain upon you by dwelling*
*on such things now. It is my painful duty to pass upon you the*
*following sentence: that you be taken from that place where*
*you are, to that place from whence you came and thence on*
*that day appointed you be taken to a place of execution, that*
*there you be hanged by your neck until your body be dead and*
*that your body will be buried in the precincts of this prison.*
*May God have mercy on your soul.*

McKenna, who had remained 'upright and dignified throughout the proceedings', collapsed in tears and had to be led from the court sobbing. Even the judge was seen to be 'visibly moved'.

John McKenna, 'aged twenty-five or twenty-six', was hung by William Marwood in Manchester on 27 March 1877, just one month and three days after his horrendous assault on his wife.

The 'haunting' of the Dawson Square by 'Poor Annie's Ghost' began in 1879 and three years later each and every one of Annie Dawson's conscious-stricken neighbours had left that blighted courtyard forever.

# CHAPTER 11

# Suffer the Little Children

The Victorians valued the 'innocence of childhood' more highly than nearly every other virtue. Yet this did not prevent the appalling treatment of young people in their mines and factories. Then, as now, there were shocking acts of violence against children; then as now these acts were sometimes premeditated, sometimes spontaneous, but as we shall see from the two following examples, they were always tragic.

Buersil Head lies about 3 miles from Rochdale in the direction of Oldham. The land, while not mountainous, is rolling and rugged; it is possible to grow crops, but only those hardy enough to thrive amongst shallow soil and rocks. Sarah Holt was born there in 1833. Her father had been a farmer-weaver and Sarah never moved far from her birthplace.

In 1857 she met Ezra Whiteoak who had lived all his life in Craven, Yorkshire and was visiting Rochdale with a friend. Ezra and Sarah were married the following year and it was agreed that the couple would take over Sarah's father's rented small-holding at Calf Hole, near Burnedge.

Ezra soon found that no matter how hard he worked the land, he could barely earn enough to support himself and his wife. When their first child, James, was born in December 1859, the Whiteoak's financial plight became serious.

The only solution was for Ezra to find a job in addition to managing the farm. Sarah, they decided, would work the land and Ezra would go to Rochdale and seek work in the mills. Ezra Whiteoak, however, had no previous experience in textiles. He was 'diligent, serious and sober,' but he still couldn't find work in the factories. The employment he found was one of the most unpleasant tasks that industrial Rochdale had to offer.

Over the previous fifty years, Rochdale had grown massively but public services had not kept pace. The streets were filthy and unpaved and the death rate was higher than almost anywhere else in the country. The average life expectancy was 23.9 years, one of the lowest in Britain. This was largely due to a lack of sanitation, particularly the absence of flushing toilets and an effective system for the removal human excrement.

In 1866, the council implemented a method of 'night-soil disposal', whereby human waste was collected weekly in pails from every house in the borough and taken to a treatment works on Entwisle Road. There, it was processed into fertilizer. The horse and cart that made the collection rounds became known locally as the 'Lavender Wagon'.

Buersil was outside the Rochdale Borough boundary, but the scheme spread rapidly and the collection process was subcontracted to a number of independent operators. One subcontractor was James Ashworth, landlord of the *Mona Hotel*, who employed Ezra Whiteoak to collect the pails from the Buersil area and transport them to Rochdale.

*'The worst job in Rochdale' – collecting 'night soil' on the 'Lavender Wagon'.*
Rochdale Local Studies Library collection

In addition to the stench, the 'Lavender Wagon' was regularly pursued by gangs of screaming children, so being a collection agent was not one of the most sought-after jobs. Still, Ezra Whiteoak had to make a living.

The birth of a second child, Sarah Anne, in May 1865, had made the Whiteoak's financial plight even worse. The farm occupied nearly nine acres, but the couple could afford only a single cow. The average ratio, even in the subsistence farming economy of Rochdale, was one cow for every three acres.

Worse, virtually nothing would grow in that soil and having abandoned an attempt at cultivating oats, the Whiteoaks reverted to a grass crop, or more accurately, stubble.

The annual rent for their smallholding was £25 per annum, a fortune given that there was virtually no revenue coming in.

Then, in February 1867, Ezra Whiteoak began to suffer from chronic rheumatism. Most of the time, night or day, he was in agony. Perched on the seat of the open wagon in all winds and weathers, hauling night-soil pails from their moorings, and straining to lift them on to the cart without spilling their repulsive contents, had taken its toll.

Ezra Whiteoak became depressed. He was a serious man at the best of times and now he was finding the stress of providing for his family intolerable. He confided to Sarah that he wished he could die, but then he 'worried incessantly about what would happen to his family if he should die before them'.

Gradually, with the coming of summer, Ezra Whiteoaks gained some measure of relief from his rheumatism and his mood seemed to improve. Nevertheless, the couple were still in financial difficulties.

Ezra managed to get a slightly higher paid and healthier job, with a local brick-maker, but it wasn't sufficient.

It was with considerable reluctance that the couple decided that their son, James, would have to start contributing to the family income. The boy was sent as a 'half-timer' to Ashworth's cotton mill.

The concept of the half-timer was a government compromise between the clamour of the reformers, who wanted to ban tiny children from working in the mills and factories, and the resistance of the manufacturers who demanded cheap labour. Thus, children were allowed to work in a factory for half a day as long as they received an education in the other half. Mornings and afternoons were alternated between work and school.

The arrangement should have worked well for the

*Half-timers crawled beneath the flying machinery in the mills to mend the yarn.*
Rochdale Local Studies Library collection

Whiteheads. As well as bringing home some desperately needed money, James was, for the first time, receiving an education.

But life in the factory wasn't easy. Children were employed as 'little piecers' in the spinning mills, crawling in the grease and oil underneath the flying machinery to tie together the 'pieces' of snapped thread.

Accidents were common; some children wedging their heads in the drive belts, others losing limbs by getting trapped between the carriage and the roller-beam. It could have been worse for James Whiteoak on his first week. He only lost a finger. The accident, however, had a profound effect on his family, particularly his father.

Sarah Whiteoak was, by the standards of the day, robust and healthy. She tilled the land, tended the cow and chopped wood. Her husband relied on her fitness and was distraught when, one evening in July 1868, she told him that she had been coughing up blood. Ezra said that he would not go to work the following morning and that they should go together to the doctor. Sarah said it was probably nothing and, in any case, they could not afford for Ezra to take a day off.

It was generally agreed that Sarah had worked wonders running the farm, bringing up the children and keeping house. The cottage was immaculate: 'whitewashed throughout, with ornaments on the dresser and a warm fire in the kitchen'. It consisted of four rooms, two up and two down, with windows to front and rear, so it was comparatively light and airy. One bedroom was used as a storeroom and 'the whole family slept in the larger upstairs bedroom'. The adults slept in a four-poster bed and the children shared a smaller bed on their parents' left.

On Monday 27 July, Ezra Whiteoak returned from work at about 7pm. He didn't say much, but then he never did. He ate a generous supper, went up to see the children, came back down and sat in his chair for an hour. The Whiteoaks kissed the children goodnight and went to bed at about ten o'clock.

Sarah was awakened at 7am by screaming. She leapt out of bed and saw her daughter, Sarah Anne, face down on the pillow. Sarah lifted the girl and saw blood oozing on to the sheets. Unable to comprehend what she was witnessing, Sarah thought that her daughter was bleeding from the mouth and attempted to wipe her daughter's chin. Then, lifting the girl's head, she saw that Sarah Anne's throat had been slashed.

To her horror, Sarah suddenly realized that her son, on the other side of the bed, also had a terrible gash to his throat. And there, slumped in the chair next to the bed, was her husband, razor in hand, blood pumping from his neck.

Sarah was beyond screaming. In mute terror she grabbed her children and half dragged them through the bedroom. Her husband caught them at the top of the staircase and pulled the razor once more across his son's neck. Somehow Sarah managed to carry her daughter downstairs and, seeing that Ezra Whiteoak had staggered back to the bedroom, laid Sarah Anne on the sofa. Her son James reeled downstairs with his father chasing him and blood splashing everywhere.

Sarah Whiteoak could bear no more and dashed the 200 yards to her nearest neighbour. The neighbour, Ann Hurst, ran nearly a mile to the *White Horse Inn* in Castleton. Having alerted the police, she, the landlord, John Ashworth and a collier named Adam Smith, sped to Calf Hole Farm.

By the time Sarah Whiteoak got back to the farm, her daughter lay dead on the sofa. Her son, James, alive, but barely, was sitting on a chair next to the sofa. Sarah climbed the stairs and her husband was sitting on the bed, blood streaming from the gaping wound in his neck. The last words his injuries would permit him to say were, 'Sarah I have done wrong.' Sarah went back downstairs.

Neighbours cautiously entered the cottage. There was blood everywhere; on the walls, the floor, the stairs and the chairs. Everyone was frozen in panic. In truth, the events were so terrible that nobody could think what to do; no one gave any assistance to James, who was getting weaker by the second.

Eventually, John Ashworth and Adam Smith climbed the stairs to the bedroom and saw Ezra Whiteoak sitting on the bed still clutching his razor. Smith grabbed Whiteoak's arm and Ashworth removed the razor from his hand. Whiteoak tried to speak but 'could only manage a low gurgling sound'.

Dr Frederick Booth arrived with the police and immediately bandaged the boy's neck, 'finding the wounds sufficient to cause death', then he went upstairs, where he found 'Ezra Whiteoak, drenched in blood, lying on the side of his children's bed, a deep gash slashed across his windpipe and gullet'.

Whiteoak's wounds looked potentially fatal but 'with his throat properly dressed, he survived to witness the death of his son downstairs'. He was led in handcuffs out of the cottage, down the lane, to the waiting police wagon.

At the subsequent inquest in Rochdale, no one could shed any light on Ezra Whiteoak's motives, least of all Whiteoak himself, who remained incapable of speech. The event was described as 'one of the most terrible to have occurred in the vicinity of Rochdale'. Ezra Whiteoak was declared to be 'of sound mind and able to stand trial for wilful murder at Manchester Assizes'.

However, although 'he was kept warm and comfortable and fed beef tea and milk through a tube', Whiteoak never stood trial for his crimes, succumbing to his wounds and dying on 2 June 1868.

Before he visited such terrible destruction on his family, Ezra Whiteoak had lived harmoniously with his wife. Isaiah Nutter did not enjoy such an amicable relationship with his wife, Mary Jane.

Isaiah and his family had moved from Haslingden to the Rochdale region and had, 'settled there amidst rancour and ill feeling'. They had moved from the centre of the town to Schofield Hall, Hollingworth Lake in early January 1879. Two weeks later Isaiah found work at Schofield Hall Mill. It was a harsh winter and for a stranger, life in the 'rough pasture, poor meadow, moorland and lofty precipices' of the Hollingworth area, must have been daunting.

Hollingworth Lake, built in 1801 as a feeder reservoir for the Rochdale Canal, was constructed by flooding a natural bowl beneath the dark hills of Blackstone Edge. Trees were planted around the lake and the lowlands were converted to pasture, which in the summer made the area an attractive place for visitors.

The railway was cut through the Summit Gap in 1841 and a halt was built at nearby Smithybridge. Tourists in their thousands flocked to the area from all over Lancashire and West Yorkshire. Many of them were millworkers, giving the lake its nickname, 'the Weighvers Seaport'. Hotels were built to accommodate the influx of holidaymakers and a paddle-steamer carried passengers from one side of the lake to the other. Rowing boats could be hired from the *Fisherman's Inn* and dances on the landing stage carried on till the early hours.

In winter, however, Hollingworth could be bleak and lonely. When the lake froze over, people would come from the neighbouring towns and villages to skate, or gallop on the ice with horses and improvised sleds; otherwise the area was virtually deserted.

A cluster of cottages adjacent to Schofield Hall overlooked the lake and it was in one of these tiny houses that Isaiah and Mary Jane Nutter set up residence. That arrangement lasted only a few weeks before a blazing row resulted in them leaving

*Steamer on Hollingworth Lake, the 'Weighvers' Seaport'.*
Rochdale Local Studies Library collection

the cottage and taking up temporary lodgings in the *Star Inn*.

The Nutters marriage had never been happy. They had fought constantly and the birth of their son, James Henry, in 1871 had made matters worse.

Whilst living in Haslingden, Mary Jane had become convinced that her husband was insane. According to her, 'he became agitated at the waxing and waning of the moon and was prone to violence on the night when the moon was full. On those occasions,' she said, 'he beat the boy badly.'

In 1877 Mary Jane left her husband and moved in with Simon Ackroyd, a Haslingden weaver. Isaiah in turn set up house with a widow called Sarah Clegg and the child went to live with Mary Jane's father, James Hays.

These arrangements lasted less than six months. Isaiah and Mary Jane who had never stopped seeing each other, visiting their son on a regular basis, gradually drifted back together. In view of the complicated scenario in Haslingden, the couple moved to Rochdale, 'in order to start afresh'.

The attempted reconciliation was a disaster. Following the row which had forced them into staying at the *Star Inn*, Isaiah was 'drinking day and night'. Mary Jane was fond of a drink as well and, being unable to find a job, spent 'much of her time in her lodgings'. Their son slept in a house nearby.

Finally, neither Isaiah nor Mary Jane could tolerate the situation any longer. On 11 February Isaiah, who could read and write well, drafted an agreement whereby he would relinquish all claim to his son who would then be legally raised by his grandfather, James Hays. Isaiah signed the paper and Mary Jane added a cross. Much to Mary Jane's fury, Isaiah then changed his mind, saying that he wanted 'to bring up his own son'.

Mary Jane still did not have work and was getting little financial support from her husband. Worse still, she had just discovered that despite of, or perhaps because of, their turbulent relationship, she was pregnant again. That night in the *Star Inn* she told her husband that she was going back to Haslingden and taking James with her to be brought up by her father. Isaiah, she said, would have to support them by 'sending a shilling or two regularly'. Surprisingly, Isaiah agreed to the proposal, but Mary Jane had little confidence that her husband would send her any money, or that the agreement he had drafted was legally binding. She insisted that they go to Henry Brierley's Solicitors' in Rochdale and get 'a proper document drawn up'.

At ten o'clock on Wednesday 30 April, Henry Brierley sat with the couple and their son to draft the contract. Isaiah Nutter told him that he and his wife had decided to live apart; she was going to take James back to Haslingden and that he, Isaiah, would have no further contact with his son.

Mary Jane said 'He beats the boy black and blue!' The solicitor turned to the boy, 'Is this true?' he asked. 'Would you prefer to stay with your mother or father?' The boy replied that he would sooner live with his father. 'He says that because his father beats him and he's frightened!' shouted Mary Jane. 'You left him and me to go with another man!' retorted Isaiah.

'You lived with someone too . . .'

'Are you both willing to sign the contract?' interrupted Henry Brierley. This they agreed to do 'and left the best of friends'.

The friendship didn't last. For the first time, the Nutters slept apart. Isaiah went to the *Fisherman's Inn* and stopped overnight with a workmate, Mary Jane slept in the *Star Inn* and James again stayed in a neighbour's house.

At about nine o'clock the following morning, Isaiah Nutter went to the *Star Inn* and asked his wife for the agreement, saying he had changed his mind. Sarah Nutter refused to give it him and another row broke out. Isaiah was escorted from the premises by the landlord and a barman. Ten minutes later Sarah, who had not seen her son since the day before, asked the landlady if she knew the whereabouts of James. The landlady replied that she had seen the boy earlier, 'playing around the corner'. Sarah Nutter walked out of the pub door to see her son in front of the *Fisherman's Inn* with her husband.

In those days there was a toll-bar adjacent to the *Fisherman's Inn* and Isaiah Nutter was leaning against a rail by the water's edge. The embankment shelved steeply to a depth of around 11 feet. Large flat-topped stones ran down the embankment and covered the bottom of the lake. By the time Mary Jane reached the rail, she could no longer see her son. 'Where is he?' she demanded. Isaiah nodded into the lake, where James was floating about 3 feet out. Screaming 'He's chucked him in the water!' Mary Jane jumped the railings, ran down the embankment, and splashed into the freezing lake. Isaiah leapt after her, overtook her, and threw the boy out further. Isaiah now stood between Mary Jane and her son. As she advanced towards him, Isaiah grabbed her by the waist, lifted her bodily out of the water, flipped her over his shoulder and immersed her head first. The

*Children paddle innocently in Hollingworth Lake.*
Rochdale Local Studies Library collection

more Mary Jane kicked, the further Isaiah pushed her down, until only her ankles and feet were out of the water.

On the embankment, Samuel Kershaw, who lived in the toll-bar, had heard Mary Jane's cry for help and spotted James floundering about 6 feet from the shore. The child was panicking, but air had permeated his clothing, keeping him afloat. Kershaw ran for a large branch that he had seen by the pub and extended it out to the boy. James had the presence of mind to grab the branch and Samuel Kershaw hauled him to the bank and pulled him ashore.

Meanwhile, as Mary Jane struggled, Isaiah Nutter slipped on one of the submerged rocks, lost his footing, released his grip on his wife and fell backwards into the water.

Coughing and spluttering, sick with fear, frozen and soaked to the bone, Mary Jane Nutter struggled out of the lake, collapsing in the arms of Samuel Kershaw who had waded in to help her.

A boat that had been launched in an attempt to rescue the

boy now went in search of Isaiah Nutter.

Hollingworth Lake, fed from the Pennine streams, which gather high up on Blackstone Edge, has some of the coldest waters in England. Even in August it is chilly, in early May it is perishing. Within the three or four minutes that it took the oarsmen to find him, Isaiah Nutter was dead.

The inquest was held the following afternoon at the *Fisherman's Inn*. Mary Jane Nutter had recovered sufficiently to give evidence, 'while her son played happily on the floor'.

The jury were instructed to reach a decision as to whether Isaiah Nutter had drowned accidentally or had committed suicide. Much was made of his wife's testimony that he was 'driven mad by the phases of the moon'. Police surgeon, Dr Hanson stated that 'although disturbing, this was by no means unusual in those of unsound mind. He was clearly mad'.

Henry Brierley, the solicitor who drawn up the contract of separation between the couple, agreed, adding that whereas Mary Jane Nutter had 'treated the matter of the separation very lightly, her husband had seemed greatly disturbed by the whole affair and did not seem to be in his right senses'.

Contrary to the advice of the Coroner, the unorthodox verdict arrived at by the jury was that Isaiah Nutter had 'accidentally drowned while attempting to take the lives of his wife and child'.

# CHAPTER 12

# The Adventure of the Steel Corset

I f the stories in the previous chapter are steeped in tragedy, *The Adventure of the Steel Corset* is tinged with farce.

The action takes place on Blackstone Edge; a grim name for a grim place, this is a moorland plateau of rough stone above Rochdale and Littleborough, criss-crossed with ancient tracks and paths. In the summer the hills can reflect the blue of the sky, in winter the colours are dominated by grey millstone grit.

Blackstone Edge has always been a formidable barrier for those travelling from Lancashire into Yorkshire. The earliest tracks and pathways were superseded by stone packhorse trails and paved roads. One stretch that could possibly be of Roman origin sweeps majestically up the Littleborough side of the hill into Rag Sapling Clough.

As trade increased, a more sophisticated and safer route into Yorkshire became imperative. The turnpike road of 1735 twisted its way through the 'craggy and dangerous terrain' to be replaced twice by more direct routes, but the climb remained arduous.

Exhausted travellers would rest at the top of Blackstone Edge, gazing back at the stunning views over Littleborough and Rochdale before beginning the second half of their journey and it was here, at the apex of the 1764 turnpike, the *Coach and Horses Inn* was built. The hotel acted as a regular stop for stage-coaches, breaking their journey to Halifax. The gradient was so steep that the climb required two additional horses being attached to the team in Littleborough. These were then detached at the inn.

In the 1830s the frequency of the stagecoaches meant that the hotel operated around the clock and became famous for miles around. But not as the *Coach and Horses*. In order to make the building visible from a distance, it had always been painted white, hence its more popular name, the *White House*.

'*Coaching days at the* White House.' Rochdale Local Studies Library collection

In 1894 the *White House* was run by landlord Peter McIntyre and his wife Ellen. The McIntyres were popular hosts. Both were described as being 'well proportioned and of a jovial disposition' – 'Fat and Jolly' in a less polite age.

In winter Blackstone Edge is cold and inhospitable. An easterly wind whips across from Yorkshire and few casual travellers take to the road. The McIntyres employed just one servant, Eliza Hill who waited on tables, cleaned and changed barrels.

It was seven o'clock on the evening of 8 December 1894, the inn was devoid of customers and Eliza Hill was polishing glasses in the taproom; Ellen McIntyre was tidying up the snug and Peter McIntyre, suffering from a heavy cold, was upstairs in bed. It was a clear night, but windy and bitterly cold. Ellen McIntyre, picking up a tankard, thought she saw a shadowy figure pass the snug window and went outside to investigate but could see nothing. She went into the kitchen and began sewing.

Eliza Hill looked up as the door of the taproom opened. A man in a wide-brimmed hat and a dark overcoat walked in and went directly to the fire.

'Cold night,' said Eliza. The stranger didn't reply; he turned from the fire, removed his hat, sat down on a bench seat and asked for three-pennyworth of whisky. He was thin-faced, dark-skinned with a three-day stubble and a piercing stare. Eliza Hill didn't like the look of him. She gave him his whisky, put the money in the secure box and joined Ellen McIntyre in the kitchen.

Half an hour later there was a crash of a chair being upturned in taproom. The stranger shouted, 'I want to see the landlord!'

Ellen McIntyre knew that, before carrying out a robbery, a thief would circle a building looking for valuables, note the exits and calculate how many people were inside. Then, if he could only see women on the premises, he would use subterfuge to establish the presence of men or dogs. 'My husband's in bed,' said Mrs McIntyre.

'I've come about the dog,' said the stranger, 'the racing dog that I paid for that you've had made up. I've come to collect it. Where is it?'

'Where's what?'

'Where's my dog and where's your husband?'

'I've told you, my husband's upstairs in bed.'

'I need to speak to him. He knows about the dog.'

'I've told you twice, he's in bed.'

'Is he very ill?'

It was clear to Mrs McIntyre that she was being interrogated by a thief.

'I'll get him,' she said.

Ellen McIntyre went through the kitchen and whispered to Eliza Hill that their 'guest' was trying to find out if there were any men or any dogs on the premises, and to prepare for trouble. Ellen went up the stairs, along the landing to the bedroom. Peter McIntyre was asleep. Ellen shook her husband awake and alerted him to the situation downstairs. Peter McIntyre may have been a big man but he dressed in flash and followed his wife down to the taproom.

The stranger was standing in front of the fire. He turned: 'You've got a dog of mine,' he said.

'I don't know what you're talking about and . . .'

'Where's *your* dog then?'

Clearly his wife had been right about the intentions of this unsavoury character. Peter McIntyre was accustomed to ejecting drunks and troublemakers; he took a step forward . . . and froze. The stranger had a revolver in his hand and was pointing it at the landlord's head.

Ellen McIntyre was halfway into the kitchen when she

realized what was happening. She leapt instinctively towards the assailant as he fired at her husband, distracting his aim so that the bullet meant for Peter McIntyre's chest smashed instead into his left arm.

It may not have been a lethal wound but it was bad enough, the bullet gouged into McIntyre's muscle and splintered the bone. The landlord slumped to his knees as the stranger took careful aim at his wife.

At that range, given the ample target, the shot should have been fatal. The assailant squeezed the trigger; there was a deafening crack, a spit of flame and Ellen McIntyre staggered backwards, hit. Then miraculously she recovered, pulled her husband to his feet and stumbled into the kitchen where Eliza Hill was hiding behind the dresser. Ellen grabbed Eliza and the two women put their weight against the door while Peter McIntyre attempted to staunch the flow of blood from his shattered arm.

'Move away from the door or I'll shoot the lot of you!'

Ellen McIntyre bolted the door and the three clambered on to the kitchen table and one by one attempted to scramble to safety through the kitchen window.

Peter McIntyre went last. It would not have been easy for the landlord to have squeezed through the gap at the best of times but now, the more furiously he tried to wriggle his way out, the more agonizing the pain in his injured arm. And he could hear his attacker breaking through the kitchen door. With a final twist, Peter McIntyre squirmed over the window ledge and tumbled on to the gravel path. He pulled himself painfully to his feet and the three ran to the side of the inn.

Clouds were now scudding across the moon and the biting wind penetrated their indoor clothes. They jumped into a gulley about 100 yards from the *White House*, lay flat and listened for any sound of pursuit.

The ditch was filled with icy water and Eliza, partly through fear and partly because of the cold, began shivering. She started sobbing. Peter McIntyre was losing blood rapidly, slipping in and out of consciousness and groaning.

Ellen McIntyre tried to quieten them both, comforting her husband with one arm and keeping Eliza warm with the other. She heard the back door of the pub swing open and bang against the wall. She whispered to Eliza to lie low, but the terrified girl panicked, stood up and began walking towards the inn. She was intent on skirting around the back of the pub, slipping on to the highway and running down the incline to safety.

The clouds parted and the moon cast a brilliant light on the girl's white apron. Ellen McIntyre watched in horror as a figure emerged from the darkness and put an arm round the servant's throat. In his other hand was a revolver, which he forced into the girl's temple: 'Tell me where the money is, or I'll shoot your brains out!' Eliza Hill's knees buckled. She begged for mercy, but the stranger, grinding the gun into her head, said: 'There's not just me here. There's three others will get all of you if we don't get the money.' 'Upstairs!' was all that Eliza Hill could manage. Then, to her relief, the grip around her neck loosened and the pressure from the gun disappeared. She turned and, in the moonlight, saw her assailant running towards the front door of the *White House*. All she could think of was escape and she fled across the main road, on to the moor and away down the hill.

Ellen McIntyre was petrified. According to their attacker, there were as many as four armed robbers prowling around the inn. Apart from a dull ache around her midriff, Ellen felt fine, but her husband was shaking and bleeding profusely. She needed to reach the highway to seek help. Not only was the night getting colder, but the clear skies were gone; a thick fog drifting up from the Yorkshire side. Ellen crept to the road under the cover of the rising mist.

The pub was disappearing in the fog when she heard the muffled sound of horses' hooves coming slowly up the hill. Her first instinct was to run for cover. Here, surely, were the stranger's accomplices come to murder them all. Then, emerging from the gloom she saw a horse and trap, and there to her enormous relief, sitting high on the seat, was Robert Gledhill, a coach driver from Littleborough. 'There's murder!' Ellen hissed and glancing fearfully over her shoulder hauled herself up beside Gledhill. 'Drive!' she implored, telling her rescuer the details only as they sped down the hill to Littleborough.

Sergeant Gilbody at Littleborough police station couldn't believe his ears. He had passed the *White House* earlier that evening and had been tempted by the peaceful glow from the lamps inside. Now, it seemed, he was to be engaged in a manhunt there.

Under instructions from Superintendent Heywood at Rochdale, Gilbody telephoned every police station within a 6-mile radius of Littleborough; then, putting his regulation pistol in his belt, he set off with two constables to meet Heywood at the *White House*.

The lights from the pub flickered dimly through the mist. The two constables crept around the back, while Sergeant Gilbody, gun in hand, walked through the front entrance. A quick search revealed that the inn was deserted. Oddly, the thief or thieves had failed to locate jewellery and some £50 in cash hidden in a bedroom cupboard and had taken nothing.

Two doctors Dr Douglas and Dr Shield from Littleborough had been alerted and, when the building was declared safe, they carried Peter McIntyre upstairs to the bedroom. He was, according to Dr Shield, 'in a weak and fainting condition. The humerus of his left arm was smashed and blood was flowing profusely from the wound'.

The two doctors extracted the bullet, which was 'fearfully large, about the size of a rifle shot' and 'having staunched the copious bleeding', bandaged the landlord's arm.

Ellen McIntyre was stood by her husband's bedside when Superintendent Heywood entered the room and asked in a puzzled voice: 'Didn't you tell the coach driver you were shot as well?'

'Yes,' the landlady replied, 'I received a blow, but, although it staggered me, there was no bleeding.' Dr Shield looked up from his patient and gave Mrs McIntyre a candid appraisal. 'Pardon my indelicacy,' he said, 'but are you by any chance wearing a corset?'

'Yes,' replied Ellen McIntyre.

'Then that's it!' said the doctor, 'the bullet has ricocheted off the steel in your corset, shaking you, but leaving you otherwise unharmed!'

And so, indeed, it was.

The police began scouring the area outside the *White House*, searching for clues. The more Superintendent Heywood scrutinized the ground, the more convinced he became that only one man had been involved. He interviewed Mrs McIntyre again and turned to his sergeant: 'He's on his own,' he said.

The description of the attacker provided by Ellen McIntyre was excellent. Superintendent Heywood was about to go through the tedious process of alerting every police station in the area once more, when fortune smiled on him.

One or two regulars had drifted into the *White House*, attracted initially by the excitement, but persuaded to stay by the fact that the redoubtable Mrs McIntyre was prepared to serve them beer. One of these customers was Edwin Clough, a farmer from the Oldham side of the hill, who remarked loudly that 'although at this time of the year you'd expect hush, the birds on the moors in the direction of Derby Bar were making a rare old row'.

Hearing that, Superintendent Heywood was confident enough to concentrate his resources. It was a filthy night, but he telephoned the sub-stations on that side of the moor to press every available officer into special duty. They were to form a cordon and walk without torches to the edge of the moor and wait, either for the suspect, or for dawn.

The police gathered at Derby Bar and silently fanned out in twos over the track. The fog swirled around them as they struggled to keep their neighbouring pair in sight. A hazy dawn broke at about 8am, and the police cordon began to move in to scour the open moorland. The men were cold, their capes were dripping wet and the moor stretched in front of them as far as the eye could see. It seemed hopeless.

Then, suddenly out of the lifting mist, Sergeant Ross from Milnrow and Sergeant Davis of Shaw spotted a figure emerging from a shallow valley to join the road in front of them. The description of the assailant matched the solitary figure on the moor and the two officers followed at a distance.

A pair of constables joined them as the road passed though a gulley at Higher Bridge, Booth Dean. The two constables left the track and overtook the suspect, cutting off the man's escape front and rear. As they challenged him, their quarry reached into his coat pocket and withdrew a heavy revolver. The gun was wrenched from his grasp and the prisoner was handcuffed and frogmarched over a mile to the police wagon.

When cautioned, the suspect replied: 'Aye, it's right, I'll make no resistance.'

Sergeant Ross opened the revolver to find it contained five rounds of live ammunition.

Once in the police cells at Littleborough, the prisoner broke down and confessed. He was, he said, 'Roger Ackrigg from Skipton, aged about twenty-five.' He was 'patrolling the Lancashire/Yorkshire border, completely alone, on the look-out for opportunities'.

Much to the amusement of his captors, Ackrigg 'proceeded to feign madness', first pretending to eat his clothes, then attempting to climb the walls of his cell and then shouting: 'Shoot 'im! Shoot 'im!' at anyone who walked past his cell. The police doctor said: 'Far from being mad, the prisoner is in good health, both mentally and physically.'

A special session of the County Bench was convened at

Rochdale Town Hall. Long before the court opened, South Parade and the Esplanade were thronged with people. They had been disappointed earlier as the police had managed to transfer Ackrigg in secret from Littleborough to Rochdale but now they jostled for a glimpse of the perpetrator of the 'Blackstone Edge Outrage'.

The doors of the court opened at 2.30pm and the crowd flocked in, fighting to get the good seats in the public gallery. Soon they were crushed in like 'herrings in a barrel and were shouting in great good humour'.

Hundreds of disappointed voyeurs were locked out and stood 'in angry knots along the passageway'. The proceedings were delayed and 'several people began stamping their feet, shouting: "Why are we waiting?!"'

Two police officers were sent upstairs to restore order, 'which they did quickly and effectively with only a minor show of force'.

*The* White House *at the time of the 'Adventure of the Steel Corset'.*
Rochdale Local Studies Library collection

Peter McIntyre was not well enough to attend the hearing, but his wife gave evidence. She related the events of the night of the attack, 'pausing occasionally to glance at the accused'. Roger Ackrigg looked very different from the desperate character that had attacked her that night. He was shaved and clean, his hair was combed and he wore 'a cream-coloured knitted scarf neatly tied around his neck and a rather good cloth suit'. Ellen McIntyre had no hesitation, however in identifying Ackrigg as 'the man who shot my husband'.

Ackrigg was committed for trial at Manchester Assizes.

At the subsequent hearing, it was revealed that Ackrigg, 'known around Skipton as a dangerous character', had served in the Royal Artillery but had fallen on hard times. He could easily access firearms but 'so far as anyone knew, had never shot at anyone before'. He was charged with 'attempted murder and attempted robbery'.

Both the McIntyre's were called to give evidence, but Peter McIntyre's memory of the incident was hazy and it was left to his wife to provide details of the incident. Peter Ackrigg, who 'stood throughout with a soldierly bearing', was found guilty and sentenced to twelve years' hard labour.

The McIntyre's returned to the *White House* celebrities. A local waxworks proprietor offered to buy Mrs McIntyre's life-saving corset to display on 'a specially prepared and entirely life-like model of her'. She 'politely but firmly, refused'.

# CHAPTER 13

# A land Fit for Heroes

Politicians told the public that the First World War would be over in twelve months. In Britain, they said, it would be 'business as usual'. They declared that the armed forces were fighting 'The War to End All Wars' and promised that when it was over, the combatants would return to 'A Land Fit for Heroes'. None of this was true.

Nearly three-quarters of a million fighting men failed to return from the conflict and those that did were given a civilian 'demob' suit, a pair of medals, a small cash payment and 'a few kind words'. Many searched in vain for employment; others too badly injured or traumatized to work were given a small disability pension. Forty-four per cent of all enlisted men ended as casualties of war.

The survivors were sorely disappointed by the peacetime world to which they returned. For many, hopes and expectations were dashed within weeks. No matter how valorously they had served their country, the skills and survival techniques learned in wartime were useless. There was one similarity, however: in peacetime as in war, it was a case of adapt or die.

Local ex-servicemen James Clarke, Joseph Buckley and Tom Widdop found the transition from conflict to peace exceptionally difficult.

James Clarke was born in Winsford, Cheshire in April 1894. He moved to Rochdale in 1913 and worked, firstly as a farm-labourer and later as a labourer for William Tatham and Sons, engineers. He moved to Clyde Street off Vavasour Street in Rochdale and married in August 1915. Only two months later he enlisted in the 'Rochdale Pals' regiment, the 6th Battalion, Lancashire Fusiliers. Clarke was sent to the Western Front, where he quickly rose to the rank of Regimental Sergeant Major. Just nine days before the armistice that drew hostilities to an end, James Clarke was involved in one of the war's final acts of heroism at Happegarbe, near Le Cateau in northern France.

He led a platoon up a heavily fortified ridge, single-handedly

*Recruitment drive in Rochdale town centre for the 'War to End All Wars'.*
Rochdale Local Studies Library collection

bayoneting the defending crews and capturing four machine-
guns. He battled on, taking three more machine-gun posts and
forty prisoners. Then, when it looked as though the remnants of
his platoon were getting bogged down, he drove a tank across an
exposed plateau and broke through the enemy lines.

Two days later, during an attack on the strategically
important Oise Sambre Canal and under a constant barrage of
gunfire from defending troops, James Clarke charged forward at
the head of a Lewis gun team, set up his weapon and took out
the enemy positions. Clarke's company advanced and the canal
was secured.

James Clarke won the Victoria Cross for his actions in the last
weeks of the war. His citation read: 'Throughout all the operation
RSM Clarke acted with magnificent bravery and total regard for
his personal safety, setting an inspiring example to all ranks.'

Clarke returned to Rochdale a hero; on 1 February 1919, a huge crowd greeted him outside the Town Hall and the following week he was presented with his Victoria Cross at Buckingham Palace by King George V.

Over the next few years Clarke picked up a succession of odd jobs, including casual labourer and stoker at an engineering factory, but he had begun drinking heavily. He had a wife and three children to support and his health was deteriorating. The jobs dried up, but the alcohol didn't. By 1930, a desperate James Clarke could be seen pushing a battered barrel organ around the streets of Manchester.

With Christmas 1930 approaching, Clarke, still unemployed, suffered a breakdown. PC William Swift was on traffic control duty at the junction of Drake Street and South Parade Rochdale when he was approached by a dishevelled James Clarke carrying a sturdy piece of wood. 'You are fully employed aren't you?' Clarke asked. 'Yes,' replied PC Swift. 'I will find you something more to do,' said Clarke.

He walked across South Parade and swung his weapon at the window of an optician's shop. The glass shattered and Clarke moved to the jeweller's next door. He smacked the stick against the glass but it bounced off and PC Swift grabbed Clarke by the arm and marched him off to the police station in the Town Hall.

'I am out of work, a victimised man,' said Clarke by way of explanation.

James Clarke appeared before the magistrates on Wednesday 17 December 1930. The Great War had been over for twelve years and the Bench was in no mood to hear tales of Clarke's heroic past. When he tried to put his vandalism into context, he was interrupted by the Chairman: 'We don't want to hear about that; confine your remarks to this case.'

Clarke persisted however, recounting a previously unknown aspect of his military service. In August 1917, he had visited an 'estaminet' – a wine and coffee shop – had got drunk and ended up in fight over a card game. He was court-martialled and sentenced to twelve months' imprisonment. On his release he was denied leave and drafted in for the final push against the Germans, during which he won his VC.

Clarke told the court he had been unemployed for six months; his wife was ill and, if imprisoned, he could lose his army pension of £10 a year. He would, he said, compensate the owner of the shop for the damage he had done.

The magistrates heard next from Chief Inspector Whiteside

*Sergeant James Clarke, VC.* Rochdale Local Studies Library collection

who had encountered Clarke before. 'He is a VC and says he has some grievance or other,' said Whiteside. 'He has been feted in the town as a hero and has taken advantage of it. He is fond of a drink and has certainly abused some of the generosity extended to him.'

Despite this less than glowing character reference, the magistrates did not jail James Clarke. They fined him 10 shillings, ordered him to pay for replacing the window-pane and sent him on his way with a stern warning.

Three years later and Clarke was arrested again, this time in London for 'obstructing a footpath'.

Nowadays actions like these would be recognized as 'cries for help' but there was no counselling for trauma victims in those days.

However, although James Clarke may have suffered a sad decline, he did not disintegrate as dramatically and with such terrible consequences as did Joseph Buckley of Whitworth.

Joseph Buckley was the son of John Buckley from Longacres Road, Whitworth, a narrow track leading to Longacres Farm and thence to the open moors at the foot of Brown Wardle Hill. In October 1914 Joseph, who had lived with his family in the cottage at number ten all his life, volunteered for service in the Royal Field Artillery. He was sixteen, too young to enlist but like many others, he lied about his age.

Buckley's early movements on the Western Front mirrored those of James Clarke. Then in June 1916, he was transferred to the Somme.

The Battle of the Somme began on 1 July 1916 and lasted until 18 November when it was called off as an unqualified disaster. Fighting on a 20-mile front, the British army lost 58,000 troops on the first day of hostilities alone.

In September 1916, the British employed tanks in an abortive attempt to push forward over the tangle of barbed wire and into enemy territory. The Germans responded with a massive shelling of the British positions and Joseph Buckley was struck on the right arm by a piece of flying shrapnel. The wound was serious. Buckley did not lose his arm, but for the rest of his short life, it hung uselessly by his side. He was invalided out of the service and returned to Whitworth in October 1916.

Later that year Joseph Buckley's two brothers were killed on the Western Front.

With his injured arm, Joseph could pick up only the most menial jobs. From September 1917 he worked as a general labourer and cleaner at Whitworth's Bridge Mills. Here he met Mary Ann Standish, a war widow whom he married in January 1918.

The Buckleys set up house at 547 Back Market Street Whitworth, the household comprising Joseph, the new Mrs Mary Ann Buckley and fifteen-year-old Minnie Boycott. Mary Ann was pregnant and gave birth to a boy six months later.

Mary Ann Buckley had known Minnie Boycott for over a year. She had given the girl a roof over her head and found her employment at Facit Mill. Minnie was originally from 8 Jermyn Street, Wardleworth in Rochdale, the eldest of eight children. Her father, William, had joined the Lancashire Fusiliers in May 1917 and had left his children, not in the care of their mother, who he considered 'not a fit and proper person' but in the custody of Inspector Furner of the NSPCC. Minnie had escaped from this odd arrangement into the informal guardianship of Mary Ann Buckley.

On 1 April 1919 Minnie Boycott caught the train to Rochdale and was crossing South Parade when, to her amazement, she literally bumped into her father. William Boycott had been demobbed and was endeavouring to re-establish his family, minus his wife. Obviously, he said, he needed Minnie to return home and help him look after her brothers and sisters. With great reluctance Minnie agreed. However, she said, because she feared she was coming down with a severe cold, she would not rejoin her family until Saturday 12 April.

Minnie Boycott returned to Whitworth and told the Buckleys of her imminent departure. She was devastated. So, it seemed, was Joseph Buckley who began behaving 'in a bizarre and erratic manner'. He failed to return home from work the following evening and went missing for the next three days, explaining on his return that he had been to see an uncle in Windsor. It was news to Mary Ann Buckley that her husband had an uncle in Windsor.

This mysterious disappearance also lost Joseph his job, his manager telling him, 'only men who could be relied upon were wanted at Bridge Mills'. Joseph Buckley was shattered; his behaviour becoming more unpredictable by the day. On 7 April Mary Ann gave him a new pair of socks she had bought in Rochdale. 'I will never wear these,' said her husband. He asked Mary Ann if she was tired of living. 'No,' replied his wife, 'I've too much to do.'

Minnie Boycott's cold cleared up and the date of her return to Rochdale loomed. On the day before her planned departure

*Market Street Whitworth, near the home of Joseph and Mary Ann Buckley.*
Rochdale Local Studies Library collection

she was 'quiet', while Joseph Buckley was, according to his wife, 'strange in every way'.

Nevertheless, on the afternoon of Saturday 12 April, Joseph Buckley sent a telegram to William Boycott to expect his daughter's return that evening. The Buckleys and Minnie had tea together and Minnie went out to get a bottle of orangeade. She returned, put the heavy stone pop bottle on the sideboard and went to her room to start packing. At 6.30pm Joseph Buckley left to go to meet his father and some friends for a drink at the Conservative Club, about 150 yards from Back Market Street.

Mary Ann Buckley was going into Rochdale for the evening and made her farewells to Minnie Boycott. 'I'll be gone by the time you get back,' said Minnie.

On her way to the station Mary Ann Buckley slipped into the Conservative Club to see her husband. 'Do you want to come to Rochdale with me?' she asked. Joseph said he'd rather stop where he was and Mary Ann left alone. Her husband played a game of billiards, and then went with his father to the *Bridge Inn*.

Mary Ann Buckley returned home on the 10.25pm train from Rochdale. The door to 547 Back Market Street was fastened, but, unusually, the key was in the lock outside. With some trepidation May Ann opened the front door. The gas was still on and the house was lit.

She called out. There was no response, but then she hadn't really expected any. Her husband had gone drinking with his father and Minnie had packed her things and left. But something was amiss. Mary Ann walked to the kitchen table and gazed in surprise at a pile of silver and copper coins. On top of the heap of coins were three letters in her husband's awkward left-handed writing.

Mary Ann picked up each in turn and read their contents with growing disbelief:

*Dear Wife,*
*I am going to end it all and I am leaving all for you. All the money and other effects I leave to you and no one else must have any insurance money but you. I hope my father and mother will have no objection as you will want all you can get to live on and bring up our child. So goodbye and god bless you.*
*Your Loving Husband, Joe.*

★

*My Dear Wife,*
*Me and Minnie have decided to end it all together after what has happened and I hope someone will look after you as you have been a true and good wife to me. You could not have been better but I am miserable with being out of work and depressed.*
*Your Loving Husband, Joe.*

★

*My dear father and mother.*
*Just a line for the last time. Things have turned out very bad and me and Minnie have done wrong and have decided to end it all together. I hope you will forgive me.*
*From your miserable son Joe.*
*I hope you will think well of Mary as she has been a good and true wife to me. So God bless you.*

Fearing the worst, Mary Ann Buckley ran up the stairs and into Minnie's room. To her relief, there was no one there. However, she was puzzled to see Minnie's clothes, which had been packed for her departure, neatly folded away in a half-open drawer. But where was Minnie? And where was Joseph Buckley?

Horace Butterworth from Facit could answer the first of those questions. At 10.45 that evening he had taken his girlfriend home and was walking down Mid-Longacres Road when he heard a groan. There, in the moonlight was a young girl, her hair matted with blood, lying face down on the side of the footpath. Beside her was a stone pop bottle.

Horace Butterworth managed to drag the girl to the surgery of Dr O'Brian. She was still alive but 'in a serious condition'. The doctor recognized Minnie Buckley and had her taken by motor ambulance to Rochdale Infirmary. There Dr Edward Cox treated her for 'shocking injuries to the head and face'.

Early next morning Minnie Boycott died as a result of 'multiple fractures to the vault and the base of the skull'. The blows that caused her death were, in Dr Cox's opinion, delivered by 'some blunt heavy weapon'.

The police mounted a search for Joseph Buckley. They interviewed his drinking companions who expressed astonishment at the turn of events. Buckley's father, John who had drunk with his son at the *Bridge Hotel* until about 9.10pm had found Joseph's behaviour, 'entirely normal'.

Joseph Buckley had returned to the Conservative Club. There he had played cards with John Sutcliffe and two other friends until about 10pm. When he left to return home to Back Market Street he was described as being 'sober and in good spirits'.

Inspector Clarke from Rochdale led the search for the missing man. They began at Mid-Longacres Road where Minnie Boycott had been found and walked north past John Buckley's cottage at 10 Longacres, up the lonely track to the high moors. About a quarter of a mile from the murder scene was New Lodge, a deep mill pond supplying *Spring Bank Mills*. At 1.30am on the top of the steep embankment the police found Joseph Buckley's gloves and cap.

At 7.30 on Sunday morning police dragged the lodge and discovered the body of Joseph Buckley.

The inquest on Minnie Boycott and Joseph Buckley took place at Rochdale Infirmary on Tuesday 15 April; Eric

Molesworth, the Deputy County Coroner, hearing evidence from Buckley's widow and father, Minnie Boycott's father; Buckley's drinking companions, Horace Butterworth, Inspector Clarke and Dr Cox.

Mary Ann Buckley expressed total disbelief at the clandestine affair, which had allegedly taken place under her roof. She had, she said, not the slightest suspicion of her husband's infidelity.

The Deputy Coroner was of the opinion that the fatal assault took place between 10pm when Joseph Buckley left the Conservative Club and 10.45pm when Minnie Boycott's body was discovered.

The jury's verdict of: 'Wilful Murder and Suicide' came as no surprise but the Deputy Coroner admitted that there were many troubling questions left unanswered by the process.

Where, for instance, had Joseph Buckley been during his mysterious three days' absence? No uncle had been traced in Windsor. And why was his wife not more concerned at his disappearance?

Was Buckley perhaps so devastated that his secret liaison was ending that he left home to commit suicide, returning only because his nerve had failed? He was, after all, sufficiently distressed to ask his wife if she had ever contemplated killing herself. And he was right in predicting that he would never wear the new socks Mary Ann had given him.

Did Mary Ann Buckley know about the affair and did that explain her apparent lack of concern at her husband's absence?

And what are we to make of the behaviour of Joseph Buckley and Minnie Boycott on the night of the murder/suicide?

Clearly Minnie Boycott did not set off to return to her family in Rochdale; her clothes were carefully replaced in her bedroom drawer. Did she wait for the return of Joseph Buckley from his night out because the two had entered a suicide pact? Or did she perhaps think that Joseph had successfully negotiated with her father that she should stay in Whitworth?

As for Joseph; why did he wait until 10pm to leave the Conservative Club? The timing was exceptionally tight. He had to get home, leave the letters to his wife and parents, walk with Minnie to Mid-Longacres and murder her before climbing the hill to the lodge. The pair could have encountered anyone on the road, including John Buckley making his way home from the *Bridge Inn*.

The jury noted that a stone pop bottle seemed a brutal choice of instrument with which to execute half a suicide pact. Was it not more likely that a pair of lovers would agree to drown together in the lodge? Perhaps Minnie Boycott, believing that she and Joseph were going for a moonlight stroll, took a drink with her, only to be fatally assaulted by her lover.

And finally, we only have Joseph's assertion in his letters that Minnie and he 'had done wrong' as evidence of an affair. The fact that Minnie Boycott did not wish to return to Rochdale does not prove that she had a sexual relationship with Joseph Buckley.

Was the affair all in Joseph's mind? We will never know.

On 31 October 1922, in a tragic echo of the murder on Whitworth moors, Agnes Fletcher, a 34-year-old widow was killed at Wicken Hall Printworks Ogden. The setting for the murder was as wild and windswept as the moors around Whitworth and the assassin was another depressed ex-serviceman.

Tom Widdop was a 28-year-old married man who had developed an obsession with Agnes Fletcher. Like Joseph Buckley he later drowned himself in a mill lodge, at nearby Jubilee Mill. At the inquest his mother stated that Widdop 'had never been right since serving with the army on the Somme'.

Local newspapers in the 1920s record scores of criminal offences committed by ex-servicemen. They range from incidents of drunkenness and vagrancy, such as the misdemeanours of James Clarke VC, to confused crimes of passion like those perpetrated by Joseph Buckley and Tom Widdop.

As each of these Great War veterans discovered, the public's gratitude did not last long in the 'Land Fit for Heroes'.

# CHAPTER 14

# The Hangman's Tale

From the early 1920s, the hangmen of Canada all shared a single alias. Unwilling to reveal their identities publicly, each used the pseudonym 'Ellis'.

Of all the people from Rochdale who achieved national fame, the original John, 'Hangman' Ellis, the man who had so inspired his Canadian counterparts, experienced by far the saddest and most macabre life.

John Ellis was born in 1875 at 18 Broad Lane Rochdale. His father, Joseph, kept a smallholding and the young John was expected to carry out odd jobs after school and at weekends. He hated it. He was a delicate and sensitive boy and could not bring himself to hurt an animal. He was, as he said later with conscious irony, 'completely unable to wring a chicken's neck'.

His father, who also had a hairdresser's business and an umbrella repair service, became reasonably wealthy. Joseph Ellis enjoyed a close relationship with his three daughters but he and John were constantly at loggerheads. As soon as he was old enough, John left home and found a job as a grinder and stripper at the Eagle Mill. The work was gruelling and Ellis, who was lightly built, found it exhausting.

He suffered a back injury and left Eagle Mill to work at Tweedale and Smalley's, the textile machine manufacturers. When he got married, the pressure of earning a family wage caused him increasing anxiety. Even his job at Tweedale and Smalley's became too taxing and he left to set up his own hairdressing business, at 451 Oldham Road, Rochdale.

His wife, Annie Beaton Ellis, was less than ecstatic when, 'for no reason he could ever adequately explain', John thought of a new way to supplement his income. He would apply to become a public hangman.

When he learned of his son's intentions, Joseph Ellis was appalled, threatening to disown John and cut him out of his will if he went ahead. If anything, this strengthened John Ellis' resolve and in March 1901 he wrote to R D Cruikshank, the Governor of Strangeways prison in Manchester who, impressed with Ellis at the subsequent interview, sent him for a week's training to Newgate prison in London.

There the 'pale, thin-haired candidate with the heavy, sandy moustache' completed his training, took a character and aptitude test, and on 8 May 1901 'John Ellis was added to the official list of executioners and assistants'. To his wife's dismay, Ellis spent his nights sitting at home reading and re-reading the techniques of his predecessor, William Marwood:

1. *Pinion the prisoner round the body and arms tight.*
2. *Bare the neck*
3. *Take the prisoner to the drop.*
4. *Place the prisoner beneath the beam to stand direct under the rope from the top of the beam.*
5. *Strap the prisoner's legs tight*
6. *Put on the cap*
7. *Put the rope round the neck tight. Let the cap be free from the rope to hide the face.*
8. *Executioner to go direct quick to the lever. Let down the trapdoors quick. No grease on the rope*

Ellis' initiation took place on 7 December 1901 when he assisted at a double hanging in Newcastle, for which he was paid £2, 10 shillings.

For the first few years, Ellis acted as assistant to Henry Pierrepoint: an experience neither man enjoyed. In retrospect it was obvious that Ellis was temperamentally unsuited to the task. He became emotionally involved.

John Ellis kept a detailed diary and recorded his 'shock and outrage' at the callousness of some of the condemned prisoners. John Edmunds was a 24-year-old labourer who sexually assaulted and shot dead Cecilia Harris in Abersychan near Newport in South Wales. He was hanged by Pierrepoint and Ellis at Usk on 3 July 1909. Edmunds winked at Ellis as he climbed the steps to the gallows and smiled broadly at Pierrepoint as the latter placed the cap over his head. He was, said Ellis, 'completely indifferent to his fate'.

The attitude of the condemned man had a profound effect on Ellis but the thing that worried him more immediately, was Henry Pierrepoint's drinking. Ellis was not averse to a drink himself, but he took his work extremely seriously and was dismayed to smell alcohol on Pierrepoint's breath at the Usk hanging. Taking the senior hangman to one side, Ellis advised Pierrepoint to drink less because 'it gave the public the impression he had to drink in order to do his work'. Pierrepoint was furious at being 'lectured and upbraided by his assistant'.

Their next assignment was a week later in Chelmsford and Pierrepoint, far from heeding Ellis' advice, arrived at the prison 'considerably worse for drink'. On the day before the execution, the prison officers were handing over the details of the prisoner to the hangmen, when Pierrepoint suddenly 'hurled a volley of abuse at Ellis'.

Ellis ignored the tirade but, as he later wrote: 'Pierrepoint rushed at me and knocked me out of my chair. I got up and sat back down but was again knocked off. He was going for me again when Warden Nash came in and attempted to stop him but failed and a blow struck me behind the ear.'

Although the execution on the following day was carried out 'impeccably', Pierrepoint was removed from the list of public hangmen, creating a lasting feud between Henry Pierrepoint, his son Albert, and John Ellis.

John Ellis was promoted to the position of Senior Public Executioner, at the rate of £10 a hanging.

The procedure adopted by Ellis as senior executioner was handed down through generations of hangmen: From the prison records, Ellis obtained the condemned man or woman's height and weight, and then computed the distance the victim must drop to meet the legal requirement that three cervical vertebrae be fractured or dislocated to snap the spinal cord and bring quick death. Underestimate the weight and the prisoner would not die, overestimate and he or she could be decapitated.

Ellis did not see the condemned man or woman until a few minutes before the hanging when he stepped into the death cell, quietly said, 'good morning' and strapped the prisoner's wrists.

One of his first assignments as senior hangman was to bring him lasting fame. Dr Hawley Harvey Crippen had murdered his wife Cora and fled the country with his mistress Ethel le Neve. They boarded the cargo ship *Montrose* sailing from Antwerp to Quebec. Crippen was travelling under the name John P Robinson and le Neve, dressed as a man, posed as Robinson/Crippen's son. However, the ruse did not deceive the captain of the *Montrose* who had connected the odd couple with the press reports of the murder in England and the subsequent flight of the suspects.

*John 'Hangman' Ellis outside his barber shop at 413 Oldham Road.*
Rochdale Local Studies Library

The *Montrose* was equipped with the latest telegraph technology and the captain immediately alerted Scotland Yard. Detectives boarded the liner *Laurentic*, which was sailing out of Liverpool and the much faster passenger ship arrived in Quebec before the *Montrose*. Dr Crippen and his companion were arrested coming down the gangplank, the first people to be captured by means of radio telegraphy. Crippen was tried for the murder of his wife and sentenced to death.

The newspapers recorded how 'on the dark, foggy morning of 23 November 1911, Dr Crippen smiled as he walked towards his hangman John Ellis'. In his pocket Crippen had a photograph of Ethel le Neve and requested that it be buried with him. His request was granted.

Nearly as infamous as Dr Crippen was George Smith who became known as 'the Brides in the Bath' murderer.

Ensuring that they all had generous life insurance policies and had written their wills in his favour, Smith had married and then drowned Alice Burnham, Beatrice Constance, Annie Mundy and Margaret Lofty. John Ellis' fame, or perhaps more correctly notoriety, increased with the execution of Smith on 13 August 1915.

The following year, Ellis' reputation spread over the water to the troubled land of Ireland. England and Germany were at war and Sir Roger Casement had attempted to obtain arms and equipment from the Germans to support the 1916 Easter Uprising in Dublin. The charismatic and popular Casement was convicted of treason and hanged at Pentonville by John Ellis on 3 August 1916. 'Casement,' said Ellis, 'went to his death like a soldier.'

By the early 1920s, the stress was beginning to tell on Ellis. He was drinking heavily and his behaviour at home had become erratic. In 1923 he was to receive an assignment that would plunge him deeper into depression.

Edith Jessie Thompson was 28 and with her lover Frederick Bywaters had allegedly plotted to kill her husband, Percy. In any event, Bywaters attacked Percy Thompson, stabbing him to death. Bywaters always maintained that he had performed the deed alone but Edith Thompson's role was considered so fundamental that she too was tried for the capital crime of murder.

The revelations at the trial merely served to stir up the public bloodlust. Thompson was already branded an adulteress; she now stood accused of carrying out a self-administered abortion. She had fantasized over her husband's death and it was alleged by the prosecution that she had discussed with Bywaters the possibilities of poisoning him.

There was a media frenzy surrounding the trial with the press initially demanding the death penalty for Thompson and then, when that sentence was imposed, orchestrating an equally vociferous campaign for her reprieve. Nearly a million people signed a petition to the Home Secretary for the commutation of the death penalty. Frederick Bywaters repeatedly stated that he had acted alone, but Edith Thompson's appeal was denied.

At 9am on 9 January 1923, Bywaters and Thompson were to be executed simultaneously at their respective prisons. Bywaters hanging was allocated to William Willis, Edith Thompson's, to his eternal regret, to John Ellis. Even at the eleventh hour, Thompson had expected a reprieve and was devastated as the time of her execution approached with no word from the Home Secretary. 'She was in a state of total collapse.'

As Ellis approached the condemned cell, Thompson let out a terrible cry and as he attempted to strap her wrists she had become semi-conscious and delirious. 'She looked,' said Ellis, 'dead already.' She was carried to the scaffold by the wardens and Ellis' assistants and had to be held upright on the trap while Ellis finalized the preparations. Ellis performed his duties in his usually efficient manner, the 'drop' was completed successfully but the horror was not yet over.

There were persistent reports that blood was dripping from Edith Thompson after the hanging. Pathologist Bernard Spilsbury, who carried out the autopsy, claimed that Edith Thompson was pregnant and had miscarried at the moment of her death; others said the bleeding was due to an inversion of the uterus caused by her earlier abortion, while the official line was that there was no blood in evidence and that the whole thing was a fabrication.

The ghastly affair had a profound effect on everyone who had witnessed it. Several of the prison officers in attendance were granted early retirement and John Ellis' health was ruined. He was to claim later that his bouts of depression were not directly linked to the hanging of Edith Thompson, but his family were convinced otherwise.

Ellis' troubles were compounded when, in the October of the same year, he was assigned to hang another woman, Susan Newell. Newell had strangled a newspaper boy named John Johnston, who had refused to hand over a paper to her without payment. She was executed on 10 October 1923, the first woman to be hanged in Scotland for fifty years. She refused to wear the traditional hood, obliging Ellis to look her squarely in the eye as he completed his task.

On 28 December 1923, an emotionally drained John Ellis hanged wife murderer John Eastwood at Armley prison, Leeds and immediately sent a letter of resignation to the Home Office. After twenty-three years and 134 hangings as Senior Executioner, it was over. John Ellis had always been regarded by the authorities as having nerves of steel, but in fact his success was more to do with meticulous planning: the weight of the prisoner, the length of the drop etc., than with emotional stability. In reality, Ellis had always been terrified of making a mistake. John Ellis had reached the end of his tether. His nerve had gone and he was battling with depression and alcoholism.

Unwisely, the first job he took following his resignation was as a pub landlord in Lowerplace, Rochdale. It was a disaster. In August 1924, Ellis was admitted to Rochdale Infirmary with a bullet wound to his jaw. The news was so sensational it even made the pages of the *New York Herald Tribune.*

From his hospital bed Ellis made a statement claiming that on the night of his 'accident' he was unable to sleep and that he had been cleaning his gun, which had detonated accidentally. Nevertheless, Ellis ended up in Rochdale Magistrates' Court, where he was charged with attempting suicide. He was warned to cut down on his drinking and was bound over for twelve months.

Those members of his family still speaking to him, persuaded Ellis to give up the pub and return to hairdressing. His new shop at 413 Oldham Road held a certain morbid fascination for the public but the business did not prosper.

Joseph Ellis had carried out his threat to disinherit his son if he became a public hangman and, as John Ellis now had two sons and a daughter to support, he was finding it even more difficult to make ends meet. His notoriety as: 'The Man Who Hanged Crippen' was all he had to fall back on.

In 1927 Ellis became involved in a grotesque scheme, which he was convinced would make his fortune, the dramatization of the life and death of Charles Peace.

In the late nineteenth century, Charles Peace was renowned as a clever and prolific burglar. Born in Sheffield in 1832, Peace posed by day as a travelling violinist. At night he terrorized and thrilled respectable society with a series of daring robberies and hairbreadth escapes.

Fleeing from a possible murder charge, Peace relocated to London, adopted the name John Thompson and carried on his night-time activities. One evening PC Edward Robinson spotted a light flickering in a window at 2 St John's Park. He surprised Peace in the process of burgling the property, chased him downstairs and, despite receiving five bullet wounds, held on to his prisoner until help arrived.

During his trial Peace confessed to having murdered a PC Nichols Cock in Manchester two years earlier, a crime for which an eighteen-year-old man had hung. Having attempted to escape justice by throwing himself under a train, Peace was executed on 4 February 1879.

As melodrama, the story of Charles Peace was hard to beat. John Ellis had a financial stake in the theatrical venture and, crucially a role to play on stage. What else but the hangman? The producers had spared no expense; the grand finale was a re-enactment of Peace's execution, complete with life-size mock scaffold. A contortionist/stuntman replaced the actor who played Peace during the rest of the play and John Ellis, recognizable to all with his bald head and heavy moustache, stepped forward to re-create his role of public hangman. The lever was pulled, the trapdoor opened, the contortionist wriggled and convulsed and the curtain came down.

The show was first performed at the Grand Theatre, Gravesend on 8 December 1927. 'It would be difficult to exaggerate the horror and revulsion . . .' began one first night review. The press were united in their condemnation. It was a disaster, the epitome of tastelessness.

The play could have been the blueprint for Mel Brooks' *The Producers*. Even the secretary of the Variety Artists' Federation added his voice to the cries of outrage: 'We think it is a most deplorable piece of bad taste. No object can be gained by pandering to such morbidity of audiences. The public are partly to blame. Presumably they all wanted to see the hanging.' Not enough of them wanted to see the hanging to make the show viable, however.

Amid a continuing barrage of protest, *The Life and Adventures of Charles Peace* closed, leaving Ellis with a huge financial loss. The one thing he did manage to salvage from the fiasco was the mock scaffold.

John Ellis had been described in the press as 'an ordinary man accepted by his neighbours'. He was usually quiet to the point of shyness, but his behaviour was becoming increasingly bizarre and unpredictable.

He began selling towels in local pubs, stopping for several drinks in each, but, deep down, Ellis still felt he could extract some financial gain from his notoriety. In a final desperate attempt to cash in on his past, Ellis took the scaffold from his failed theatrical enterprise out on the road.

His travelling show was not a dramatization of a single event; it was optimistically billed as 'a scientific and accurate reconstruction of the techniques of the hangman'. Ellis appeared at fairs and seaside shows, dressed in a heavy black suit and tie, his moustache bristling as he paced the stage, waving his arms and recalling the deaths of Crippen, Casement and Thompson.

At the end of each 'show', with a tug of his lever, Ellis would send a dummy crashing through the drop, to swing grotesquely in front of a disbelieving audience.

Ellis may not have been a laughing stock, his new career provoked revulsion not laughter, but he was operating at the lowest end of the entertainment spectrum. Sideshows got no tackier or more distasteful than this. Neither was there the appetite for public hanging, real or facsimile, which had existed in the times of Tyburn or the New Bailey at Salford. The shows were not a success.

These constant reminders of his past did nothing to improve Ellis' state of mind, or to reduce his drinking. The economic depression of the 1930s was hitting Rochdale hard. The textile industry was in decline, thousands were out of work and people, finding it a struggle to find money for food, were not going to squander it on haircuts. The barber's shop now brought in next to nothing. In the final irony of Ellis' sad life, it was to be the tools of his failing trade which were to end his life.

On 19 September 1932, following a day's work at the hairdressers', John Ellis returned home, ate his tea, and for no apparent reason, trapped Annie, his wife, in the kitchen and threatened to 'cut off her head' with a cut-throat razor. Annie ran out of the house as their daughter Amy walked in to the room. Her father shouted: 'I can't cut off your mother's head, so I will cut off yours!' Fortunately for Amy, at that moment, her mother returned with Ellis' son, Austin. But as Austin walked towards his father, John Ellis, in a last gesture of despair drew the razor blade across his own throat. PC Clarke, the first policeman to arrive on the scene found the former hangman, 'lying face down on the floor in a pool of blood'.

John Ellis was taken to Rochdale Infirmary where he died on the following day.

In a final twist to this macabre tale, the Canadian hangman who, out of respect for John Ellis, first adopted the Rochdale man's surname for his pseudonym, in his turn bequeathed his alias to the annual award of the Canadian Crime-writers' Association. These are known as the Arthur Ellis Awards and the winning trophy is a wooden hanged man, 'who dances when the string around his neck is pulled'.

*John Ellis takes his show on the road.* Rochdale Local Studies Library collection

CHAPTER 15

# The Booby Trap Bomber

I t was 20 March 1941. Britain was at war. The so-called 'phoney war' – an uneasy calm before the storm – was coming to an end. There was a sense of excitement, of foreboding and a very real fear of invasion. Amongst the young especially, there was a widespread fascination with everything military: aeroplanes, fighting vehicles and weaponry.

It was cold and damp that evening in Rochdale. The nights

*Town Hall Square – the war effort in 1940.* Rochdale Local Studies Library collection

were drawing out but a blackout was in force and by eight o' clock it was dark. Five men walked briskly up Yorkshire Street, across Cheetham Street and along Whitworth Road, their coat collars turned up and the brims of their hats shading their faces against the rain. Four were detectives from the Rochdale Constabulary; the fifth rented a cellar workshop beneath a grocer's shop at 58 Whitworth Road.

Sometime between 16 and 18 November the previous year, there had been a robbery from a military munitions store adjacent to a gymnasium on Hudson Street. Amongst items missing from the store, were a Thompson submachine-gun, 1,200 rounds of ammunition and twelve hand grenades.

The police were worried. The prospect of this material being used by criminal elements was the stuff of nightmares. Worse, the breach of security was so bad that there even some doubt as to the total amount of weaponry removed from the store.

Several raids had been carried out on premises in Rochdale, but although police did uncover a cache of illegal handguns, none of the missing mini-arsenal from Hudson Street was found. Four months passed without a word as to the whereabouts of the arms then on the afternoon of 20 March 1941, an anonymous informant told detectives that there were guns hidden in the cellar of 58 Whitworth Road. The police obtained a search warrant and interviewed William Bury, who rented the cellar. Bury denied any knowledge of the stolen weapons. He was ordered to bring the keys to the workshop and accompany the police to the premises.

So seriously did the Rochdale police take the situation that four top detectives were assigned to the task: Detective Inspector Stables, Detective Sergeant Dale, Detective Sergeant Faulkner and Detective Constable Scade. Having gained entry to the ground floor, Inspector Stables ordered a search of cupboards and storerooms. The search uncovered boxes of tangled electrical equipment but no weapons.

William Bury opened the cellar door, switched on the light and the five men descended the whitewashed stone steps.

The cellar was divided into three sections. The first was filled with cartons and discarded electrical items but as Inspector Stables ducked under the archway into the second area, he noticed that one of the flagstones was slightly out of alignment, as if it had been recently moved. Sergeant Dale knelt down and lifted the flag and there in a rectangular hole dug into the earth beneath the flagstone, was a large wooden crate.

*Basement premises, Whitworth Road, near the booby-trapped cellar.*
Rochdale Local Studies Library collection

The box was covered in creosote and pitch and was wedged firmly into the ground, so although it had ropes on each side, the officers were unable to budge it. They had come prepared with tools; the lock on the box was broken and DS Dale lifted the lid. Whatever was inside had been carefully covered by a piece of felt. Sergeant Dale looked up at Inspector Stables who was crouching behind him and gently lifted the felt. Underneath was another equally neat piece of folded material.

As Sergeant Dale began to move the second layer of felt, a deafening explosion ripped through the cellar. The room was plunged into darkness and the sound waves pulsed and echoed in the blackness.

Detective Sergeant Faulkner had been stood behind Sergeant Dale and was thrown by the force of the blast back through the archway into the first section of the cellar. He was totally disorientated but miraculously, uninjured. Above the terrible ringing in his ears, he could hear groans and cries from around the corner. He pulled himself upright and gradually his eyes adjusted to the dark.

Constable Scade was slumped against the wall clutching his arm and William Bury was on his knees with his head in his hands. Then Faulkner saw two bodies on the floor. It was obvious that the men lying beside the box were seriously hurt. Sergeant Dale had taken the full force of the explosion and Inspector Stables was also in a very bad way. Sergeant Faulkner climbed the stairs into the shop and alerted the police and ambulance services.

The injured men were taken to Rochdale Infirmary. Detective Sergeant Dale had died within minutes of the explosion; Detective Inspector Stables succumbed to his injuries in hospital the following morning. William Bury, who had received serious head wounds, lost his right eye during surgery and Constable Scade suffered a broken arm and serious cuts and bruising.

The bomb squad from the Royal Engineers were called in and concluded that the men had been the victims of a sophisticated booby trap. Attached to the lid of the box and hidden in a coating of pitch, was a piece of wire, one end of which was attached to the underside of the lid. The wire had been fed through the felt to a Mills bomb, or hand grenade, and

*Bomb victim – Detective Inspector Harry Stables.* Greater Manchester Police Museum

wrapped around the pin. The pin itself was not the original but a home-made replacement that was thinner and longer and easier to slide out. When the box lid was opened, the pin was slowly removed, the lever of the grenade was released, the fuse was ignited and seven seconds later, the bomb exploded.

The contents of the box had been heavily greased to preserve them in the damp of the cellar and included a Thompson machine-gun, a .12 bore shotgun with a sawn down barrel, a Winchester rifle, a Belgian shotgun, eight fully charged grenades, a Colt automatic and over 1,000 rounds of ammunition.

The town had lost two of its finest officers in the explosion. Harry Stables had served in the Royal Navy throughout the First World War and then followed his father into the police service. Thomas Dale had joined the Rochdale force in 1923 and had received five commendations for his service to the Borough. Both were married with children, each had a young son.

William Bury also had a son. Raymond Bury was eighteen, a precociously gifted electrician who worked with the radio engineers Rochdale Re-diffusion. Raymond lived with his parents at 31 Ventnor Street, off Ashfield Road but had operated independently of any parental control for years.

On Friday 16 November 1940, Raymond Bury had been to the early show at the Regal Cinema and had walked across the Esplanade, up Yorkshire Street to Toad Lane and on to Hudson Street. He was heading for the gymnasium run by his friend Bill Hargreaves. When he got there the gym was closing so he and Hargreaves walked back towards Ventnor Street.

Hargreaves told his friend that the King's Own Yorkshire Light Infantry were using another part of the premises on Hudson Street to store munitions; that the window at the back of the building had fallen out and that the window frame was boarded up with just a few pieces of light hardboard. This was fascinating news for Raymond Bury. Guns were his obsession.

In August 1940 Bury had been in an amusement arcade on Oldham Street in Manchester where he had met a soldier in uniform who claimed to be a veteran of the Dunkirk landings. Bury had asked the soldier if he had any guns to sell and the man had ushered him out and around a corner into an alley, 'near a rough hotel'. The soldier produced a Colt automatic and, after some haggling the Bury agreed to pay 15 shillings for the weapon.

Raymond Bury had rented a lock-up at Foot Mill, Shawclough where he would meet with friends and experiment with home-made electrical devices. He took the gun there and hid it amongst his electrical equipment. This was the start of Bury's weapon collection. It was soon to grow.

Raymond Bury's best friend was Ronald Rigg, who lived on his own in Church Stile near the Parish church. Rigg was slightly older than Bury and had signed up to serve in the RAF, but before he left Rochdale he and Bury had broken into Bateson's Ironmonger's on Yorkshire Street and stolen a Winchester .27 rifle and ammunition, a twelve bore shotgun, a Winchester .22 repeater, a Browning repeater, several air pistols, cartridges and pellets. These items too were hidden in Foot Mill.

When Bill Hargreaves told Raymond Bury about the military store on Hudson Street, the image of this unattended arsenal haunted Bury all that night. Early the following evening, he borrowed his father's car and visited the gymnasium again.

The premises were deserted, so Bury went to the rear of the building, easily accessing the store via the boarded window and there, just as Bill Hargreaves had described, was a treasure trove. There were boxed Thompson machine-guns lying on the floor, Bren guns on stands scattered throughout the room, boxes of grenades and scores of cartons of ammunition, stacked on shelves and folding tables.

Raymond Bury had time to walk out with the machine-gun under his coat, hide it in the car and return for some grenades and ammunition. He drove to Foot Mill and hid his plunder upstairs; then he returned his father's car and walked back to the gym. Bill Hargreaves was there, so they lifted a few weights and then Hargreaves insisted on showing Bury the munitions store. So for the second time that night, Raymond Bury saw the collection of weapons. This time he resisted temptation and both men left the building and went home.

At ten o'clock that night, Lieutenant Warren of the King's Own Yorkshire Light Infantry visited the munitions store and knocked on the door. Receiving no reply, he went around to the rear of the building and, finding the window opened, raised the alarm then climbed in and stood guard for twenty minutes until he was relieved. He returned and stayed until after midnight when an attempt was made to barricade the window.

The next morning an inventory was taken 'and various items found to be missing'. The vagueness of that description is matched by the confusion as to when the theft took place: 'between 3pm on 16 November and 10pm on 18 November'.

Raymond Bury didn't get much pleasure from his hoard of

weapons at Foot Mill. His security was better than that of the army, but not much. Friends who visited the mill noticed that he was becoming extremely nervous. He told them of suspected break-ins at the mill, which he was convinced had been orchestrated by the police, and mentioned the possibility of creating booby traps to deter uninvited guests.

Bury was 'a genius at rigging up devices'. His electricity supply at the mill came from a generator powered by a waterwheel that he had set up himself. He had talked previously about 'rigging up something which would deliver mild electric shocks' and his friends assumed he was talking about installing one or two such devices in Foot Mill; but he then hinted that his new deterrent might include the use of a grenade.

Raymond Bury became convinced that Foot Mill was under surveillance. Once again he borrowed his father's car and with the help of a friend, Joe Page, took 'all the electrical goods, some antiques and the guns' under the cover of night, to the cellar at Whitworth Road.

*Foot Mill Shawclough, where Raymond Bury hid his mini-arsenal.*
Rochdale Local Studies Library collection

The tip-off to the police on 20 March 1941 had consisted only of the address where the stolen weapons were stored, but having discounted the involvement of the injured William Bury in the theft, there could only be one suspect. At 10.15pm Detective Sergeant Brighton visited Raymond Bury at Ventnor Street and asked him if he knew anything about an explosion at Whitworth Road. Bury denied any knowledge of an explosion but was arrested on suspicion of having stolen the guns, bombs and ammunition from Hudson Street.

At the police station he said, 'I went to that place in Hudson Street, saw the gun and collared it.' It was enough. Bury was first charged with the theft of the weaponry; this was later revised to six charges of murder, attempted murder and 'maliciously causing an explosion of a nature to endanger life'.

Raymond Bury was remanded twice; the case against him was complicated. Was it murder? Had Bury intended to kill? If so, who were his intended victims?

The trial of Raymond Bury began on 20 April 1940. The defence, led by Arthur Jalland immediately made the startling claim that, although he may have indeed removed the guns and bombs from Hudson Street and set a deadly booby trap in Whitworth Road, Bury may not have been guilty of any crime under English law.

There was some doubt as to whether the entry into the army store had been forced and there appeared to be, 'no precedents to quote in relation to the setting of the booby trap with death ensuing'. *The Offences against the Persons Act* of 1861 stated that it was not illegal to set a dangerous device for security so long as the mechanism was activated during the hours of darkness. The Judge, Mr Justice Asquith was non-committal and the trial proceeded.

The case for the Crown seemed straightforward as the facts were hardly in dispute. The defence then presented a number of witnesses to provide character references on behalf of the accused and then called Raymond Bury himself to the stand. Bury revealed that the booby-trapped device was not the only deterrent in the cellar and that the electrical wiring in the third section of the room had been tampered with to give a shock to anyone switching on the wall light. His defence was that his objective all along had been to safeguard his cache, not to endanger life.

Bury's explanation for the setting of the traps was that he had intended to join the navy and wanted to protect the weapons' hoard in his absence. The reason that he had built up his collection in the first place, he said, was because 'he needed to be prepared for a possible German invasion'.

Arthur Jalland continued this theme on his clients' behalf: 'We have here a boy who has progressed more than ordinary boys in one direction, but less in others. These adolescent boys have been brought up for the last two years with talk of little but invasions. This most unhealthy atmosphere has been abetted by an almost criminal negligence on behalf of the military authorities who have enabled this young man to feed his fantasies.'

Jalland then returned to the legal complexities of the case. He referred to an incident two years earlier where a man had set up an automatic pistol to protect his pigeon cote and his son had been shot dead. The judge in the subsequent trial had ruled that the case was clearly one of manslaughter, not murder.

Mr Justice Asquith once more ordered defence counsel to proceed on the evidence in front of them. Jalland again argued that Bury's motivation had been not been malicious: 'It was significant that he buried the box in the cellar. He not only buried it but pitched it so it could not easily be removed, covered it with a stone flag and placed other boxes on top so that the place should not be discovered. He took every precaution to prevent anybody going to the munitions.'

His Lordship didn't say, 'Come off it!' in so many words, but it was close: 'How can anyone in his senses imagine that to be the case, when there was a live Mills bomb inside the box primed to go off?' he demanded.

However, the defence had clearly raised an important point of law and the judge ordered a recess. When the court reconvened Mr Justice Asquith was prepared to accept a reduced charge of manslaughter, to which Raymond Bury pleaded guilty.

During his summing up, the Judge said that having searched 500 years of precedents he had failed to come up with a parallel case. He turned to Raymond Bury and said: 'Under the circumstances, you are extremely lucky that your plea of manslaughter has been accepted. You acted with an utterly criminal disregard for human life and the result of that is that two conscientious police officers have been killed and two other people seriously injured, including your own father.' He then turned to the lack of security at the army store on Hudson Street, saying: 'If there had been the slightest elementary supervision by the military authorities this sorry state of affairs would have been avoided.'

The Judge then passed sentence: 'This is a very grave case of manslaughter. I do not think it is possible to impose on you a sentence of less than seven years' penal servitude, on each indictment, the sentences to run concurrently.'

The two corteges bearing the bodies of Detective Inspector Stables and Detective Sergeant Dale met at the junction of Sandy Lane and Bury Road. They passed between a huge Guard of Honour extending to the Cemetery gates and including officers from the police and ambulance services, the fire brigade, the War Reserve and representatives of police forces throughout the country; but no one was there from the King's Own Yorkshire Light Infantry.

# CHAPTER 16

# The Case of the Rochdale Mummy

Ashfield Valley flats in Rochdale were designed as 'beacons for the future of housing', not just locally but nationally. In July 1966, Rochdale Council's Estate's Committee approved an ambitious development based on a revolutionary Swedish prefabrication system called Skarne.

The new estate would accommodate thousands of people previously trapped in the crumbling terraces and decaying courtyards still blighting inner Rochdale. Then the bulldozers would remove the old slums and create 'a town centre which will be modern, well-designed, light and airy'.

The area where the new housing development was to be located was bleak and derelict, full of hen-coops and rubbish and divided by 'Jacky Brook' – a storm-water outflow that carried sewage in flood conditions. A total of 1,014 flats were to be built in a series of structures, which varied from two to seven storeys, dependent upon the lay of the land.

In order to access the various levels, lifts were to be installed along the blocks and the flats themselves were linked by decks running the length of each unit. This was the so-called 'Deck-Access System', designed to 'provide communal access and foster community spirit'.

The accommodation would range from bedsits to four-bedroomed flats, thus encouraging a mix of tenants and all flats were to be heated by a cheap and efficient gas central heating system.

Work began clearing the site in April 1967 and the first flats were available for habitation in June 1968. At first people loved them. Most units were larger than the tiny back-to-back houses they replaced. They looked modern and seemed more secure than the areas of dereliction and poverty in which many tenants had been born and raised. Some thought that the deck-access system made 'the Valley' look like 'a concrete prison' but initially people were content.

Unfortunately the development was 'designed by architects with an agenda, not builders with inspiration' and the dream rapidly turned into a nightmare.

The honeymoon period came to an abrupt end as the fabric of the buildings began to deteriorate. It was not the dampest housing estate in Rochdale, but it was not the driest either, with mould and fungus invading the majority of units.

The dream of improved security was also proved illusory. Vandalism became endemic with gangs able to roam unchecked along the open decks. 'A lift repaired on Monday morning would be damaged again by lunchtime.' By 1974, as a counter-measure, the lifts were shut on Sundays and even sometimes during the week.

Unemployment produced gangs of disaffected teenagers with nothing better to do than huddle in threatening groups day and night. There were complaints of open drug use, drunkenness, fighting, people sleeping in corridors and lifts being used as toilets. Properties were being unofficially sub-let;

*The new Ashfield Valley Flats.* Rochdale Local Studies Library collection

one practise in the taprooms of the local pubs was to rent a room on Ashfield Valley by the hour.

This is not the complete picture. The majority of people on the Estate were decent and hard-working and just wanted to get on with their own lives. A community spirit built up via Tenants' Associations and a number of unofficial networks and many people thoroughly enjoyed living on 'the Valley'.

It sometimes seemed that those who liked the development most were 'the young, who could enjoy a bohemian lifestyle and the old, who remembered the terrible conditions on "the Mount" or the "Paddock" in Rochdale'.

The problem was that in some areas of this vast development, people could become invisible, or simply disappear.

James Finlay was born in Southport in 1943 and lived there most of his life. He married in 1965 but the marriage was not a success and in 1971, Finlay met Eileen Willan and obtained a divorce from his first wife. James and Eileen married, relocated to Rochdale and in February 1975 the couple, who by now had two children moved into 28 Buttermere on Ashworth Valley.

James Finlay, a labourer, found employment with R and T Howarth, the Rochdale building contractor. Suddenly, without notice, he stopped coming to work, picking up his last wage packet on 29 August 1975.

By March 1977 there were substantial rental arrears at 28 Buttermere and the Housing Department of Rochdale Council, having exhausted the process of warning and final warning, issued an eviction notice on the Finlays. The property was vacated on 5 March 1977.

The ground floor refuse areas of the Ashfield Valley flats were gloomy, poorly lit and ill-smelling at the best of times. The huge metal bins, which caught refuse from the chutes connected to each flat, were a constant target for bored teenagers. On 1 March 1977, the fire brigade had been called out to extinguish a blaze in one of the 5-foot-high bins in the unit adjacent to Buttermere. The heat from the fire had cracked the electric light and the cavernous rectangular block was even darker than usual.

A week on, and the light still hadn't been replaced. A resident hurrying through the gloom with her two daughters noticed a wire shopping trolley parked against the wall adjacent to the bins. There was a large sack-like object in the trolley but the stench from either that or the bins was overpowering and she hurried her children through to the lift.

*The Ashfield valley Flats, near the site where the 'Rochdale Mummy' was discovered.* Rochdale Local Studies Library collection

The next person to visit the area also gave the package a wide berth and it was the caretaker of the flats who, on 13 March, seeing what he thought was a large sack of cement, contacted the Council's Cleansing Department.

Two men arrived the next morning to remove the package. One gave the trolley a good kick to get in nearer to the light source in the doorway; it hit a piece of wood, rocked and tipped over, spilling its contents on the floor. With growing disbelief the men realized that what had toppled out of the trolley was not a sack of cement but a body, or at least human remains. The head was covered with a plastic shopping bag and the hands and feet were tightly bound. The closest comparison they could arrive at was that it was like an Egyptian mummy; semi-preserved, solidified and covered in filthy rags

The police could only agree. There seemed to be little they could do to identify the unfortunate victim. The plastic bag over the head had encouraged millions of mites and maggots, which obliterated the face, leaving no identifying features. The torso was desiccated and partially mummified and there seemed to be no possibility of lifting prints from the blackened fingers.

The only immediate forensic evidence available to the investigating team was gleaned from the liver of the deceased. Some internal organs had been preserved by the mummification of the torso and, following a detailed forensic investigation, it was even possible to pinpoint the cause of death . . . an overdose of barbiturates, specifically *Amylobarbitone*. The process of identifying the body, however, was nowhere near so straightforward.

Then, Chief Inspector Tony Fletcher of the Greater Manchester Police Fingerprint Bureau had a flash of inspiration. On every finger except one, the skin of the deceased had deteriorated; to such an extent that the prints had disappeared completely. On the right middle finger, however, an echo of a print seemed to survive.

Writing in 1959, forensic scientist Sydney Smith had said:

*It is from the dermis, the underling true skin that the various ridges, loops and whorls that form fingerprints develop. Dermal prints remain after the epidermis has been destroyed by putrefaction or other cause, and they are an equally certain form of identification.*

Inspector Fletcher recalled this excerpt because he had recently used the theoretical construct in partnership with Manchester Museum's Department of Egyptology.

A team from the University led by Professor Rosalie David had been investigating the mummified corpse of *Asru*, a chantress at the Temple of Amun in Karnak. The corpse was over 2,500 years old but had been partially preserved by her mummification and Professor David had worked with Tony Fletcher devising a methodology for lifting Asru's fingerprints.

Rosalind David was amazed when Fletcher contacted her to employ the same methods for an ongoing investigation, *The Case of the Rochdale Mummy*. The hands were removed from the corpse and sent to the University. As with Asru, the epidermis on the right middle finger was raised, but when that layer was removed, the dermis was preserved beneath. A specially adapted, quick-drying dental putty was applied to the finger, allowed partially to set and then removed to dry thoroughly. When several layers of acrylic paint were applied to the mould, a cast was produced and a fingerprint could be obtained by the standard methods.

Inspector Fletcher could now go back to the National Fingerprint Database looking for a match. Modern fingerprint science requires sixteen points of similarity between prints to authenticate identification between two samples. The National Database produced a match from their records and provided an identity for the Rochdale Mummy . . . James Finlay.

The police soon tracked down Eileen Finlay, living with her two children, but, unsurprisingly, without her husband. She denied that the body in the refuse area was that of James Finlay and claimed that she had not seen her husband for nearly two years; but presented with the forensic evidence, she changed her mind and made a statement.

According to Eileen Finlay, in late August 1975, she and her husband had rowed more seriously than usual. On occasions, during their periodic flare-ups, James would become violent and at that point Eileen would leave the flat. This time he was maudlin as well as angry and threatened to kill himself if Eileen walked out on him. Eileen went to the bathroom cabinet, took out a bottle of tablets and threw them at her husband saying: 'Bloody well get on with it then!' The tablets were *Amylobarbitone*.

Returning to the flat after several hours in the pub, Eileen Finlay found her husband dead on the sofa, bound hand and foot. This was inconvenient to say the least, so, according to Eileen, she tightened her husband's bonds and dragged him across the room. Then, tired of seeing his dead face in the corner of the room, she put a plastic shopping bag over his head. Finally, irritated by having a corpse on display at all, she dragged her husband's body to the airing cupboard and bundled it in, to be eaten by maggots and mummified for a period of eighteen months.

The eviction notice, served on her in March 1977 finally provided the incentive to cart the body downstairs and into a shopping trolley in the neighbouring refuse area.

The police may have had some doubts as to the motivation of a man that 'hog-ties' himself after taking an overdose. They may have even marvelled at the suppleness of anyone able to achieve such a contortion, but, given her denials, the Director of Public Prosecutions was of the opinion that a conventional charge brought against Eileen Finlay would not succeed.

Accordingly she was tried on two seldom evoked criminal charges. The first was that: 'she intended to prevent the coroner of Rochdale from carrying out an autopsy on the dead body of her husband James Finlay who died an unnatural or sudden death' and the second that: 'she left unburied the dead body of her husband, for whom she was bound to provide a Christian burial and had the means to do so'.

Eileen Finlay was convicted on both counts and sentenced to two years imprisonment.

All but four of the flats in Ashfield Valley have now been demolished, replaced by the mixed use Sandbrook Business, Retail and Entertainment Park. Gone but not forgotten? Perhaps. Former residents who talk of a late-blossoming community spirit on the estate can now look back with nostalgia at their lives on the Valley, and nobody will ever forget the Rochdale Mummy.

# Bibliography

**Manuscript and Printed Material**
Home Office Disturbance Papers, Public Record Office. Kew, London
Lancaster, Liverpool, Manchester Assizes: Court Records. Lancashire County Record Office, Preston.
Census of Great England and Wales. 1841–1901
Ordnance Survey Maps. Rochdale Local Studies Library
Rochdale Council Minutes. Rochdale Local Studies Library
Rochdale Police Commissioners Minutes. Lancashire County Record Office, Preston

**Newspapers**
*Manchester and Salford Examiner*
*Manchester Courier*
*Manchester Guardian*
*Manchester Times and Examiner*
*Rochdale Monthly*
*Rochdale Observer*
*Rochdale Pilot*
*Rochdale Sentinel*
*Rochdale Spectator*
*Rochdale Standard*
*Rochdale Times*

**Books and Journals**
Cole, John, *Rochdale Revisited*, vols. 1 and 2
Fishwick, H., *History of the Parish of Rochdale*
Mattley, Robert, *Annals of Rochdale*
Heywood T.T., *New Annals of Rochdale*
Taylor, Rebe, *Rochdale Retrospect*

# Index

# TRUE CRIME FROM WHARNCLIFFE

*Foul Deeds and Suspicious Deaths Series*

| | |
|---|---|
| Barking, Dagenham & Chadwell Heath | Leeds |
| Barnsley | Leicester |
| Bath | Lewisham and Deptford |
| Bedford | Liverpool |
| Birmingham | London's East End |
| Black Country | London's West End |
| Blackburn and Hyndburn | Manchester |
| Bolton | Mansfield |
| Bradford | More Foul Deeds Birmingham |
| Brighton | More Foul Deeds Chesterfield |
| Bristol | More Foul Deeds Wakefield |
| Cambridge | Newcastle |
| Carlisle | Newport |
| Chesterfield | Norfolk |
| Colchester | Northampton |
| Coventry | Nottingham |
| Croydon | Oxfordshire |
| Derby | Pontefract and Castleford |
| Durham | Portsmouth |
| Ealing | Rotherham |
| Folkestone and Dover | Scunthorpe |
| Grimsby | Southend-on-Sea |
| Guernsey | Staffordshire and The Potteries |
| Guilford | Stratford and South Warwickshire |
| Halifax | Tees |
| Hampstead, Holborn and St Pancras | Warwickshire |
| Huddersfield | Wigan |
| Hull | York |

## OTHER TRUE CRIME BOOKS FROM WHARNCLIFFE

| | |
|---|---|
| A-Z Yorkshire Murder | Norwich Murders |
| Black Barnsley | Strangeways Hanged |
| Brighton Crime and Vice 1800-2000 | The A-Z of London Murders |
| Durham Executions | Unsolved Murders in Victorian and |
| Essex Murders | Edwardian London |
| Executions & Hangings in Newcastle | Unsolved Norfolk Murders |
| and Morpeth | Unsolved Yorkshire Murders |
| Norfolk Mayhem and Murder | Yorkshire's Murderous Women |

Please contact us via any of the methods below for more information or a catalogue.

## WHARNCLIFFE BOOKS

47 Church Street – Barnsley – South Yorkshire – S70 2AS
Tel: 01226 734555 – 734222 Fax: 01226 – 734438
E-mail: enquiries@pen-and-sword.co.uk
Website: www.wharncliffebooks.co.uk